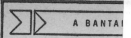 

THE GREAT CARS

Maserati, Ferrari, Mercedes-Benz, Lancia

THE GREAT RACES

Le Mans, Monte Carlo, Indianapolis,
the Mille Miglia

THE GREAT DRIVERS

Vukovich, Nuvolari, Moss, Fangio, Campbell,
Ascari, Rickenbacker

WHEN ENGINES ROAR

Thrilling true stories of the greatest moments
in auto-racing history!

WHEN ENGINES ROAR

Edited by
WILLIAM F. NOLAN
and
CHARLES BEAUMONT

BANTAM BOOKS

BANTAM PATHFINDER EDITIONS

NEW YORK / TORONTO / LONDON

RLI: $\dfrac{\text{VLM 7.0}}{\text{IL 7.12}}$

WHEN ENGINES ROAR

A Bantam Pathfinder edition / published September 1964
2nd printing

ACKNOWLEDGMENTS

"The World's Finest—Fangio or Nuvolari?" by Ken W. Purdy, reprinted from *Sports Cars Illustrated* by permission of the author. Copyright, 1958, by Ziff-Davis Publishing Co.

"Indy's Iron Man" by Frank Anmar, reprinted from *Car Life* by permission of the author. Copyright, 1962, by Bond Publishing Co.

"Roses in the Rain" by William F. Nolan, reprinted from *Car and Driver* by permission of the author. Copyright, 1961, by Ziff-Davis Publishing Co.

"Jalopies I Cursed and Loved" by John Steinbeck, reprinted from *Holiday* by permission of the author's agent, McIntosh and Otis, Inc. Copyright, 1954, by John Steinbeck.

"Racing's Roaring Age" by Russ Catlin, reprinted from *True's Automobile Yearbook* by permission of the author. Copyright, 1954, by Fawcett Publications, Inc.

"With Moss in the Mille Miglia" by Denis Jenkinson, reprinted from *Motor Sport* by permission of the Teesdale Publishing Co. Copyright, 1955, by the Teesdale Publishing Co.

"The Oldest of Them All" by W. F. Bradley, reprinted from *Motor Racing Memories* by permission of the author. Copyright, 1960, by W. F. Bradley and published by Motor Racing Publications, Ltd.

"Dark Inheritance" by Erwin C. Lessner, reprinted from *True* (as "The Man Who Inherited Death") by permission of the author's widow, Ann M. Lingg Lessner. Copyright, 1957, by Fawcett Publications, Inc.

"Australia's Mad Redex Trial" by Jeff Carter, reprinted from *Road & Track* by permission of the publisher, John Bond. Copyright, 1956, by Enthusiasts' Publications, Inc.

"The Psychology of Motor Racing" by Raymond de Becker, reprinted from *Annual Automobile Review* (Automobile Year) by permission of the editor, Ami Guichard. Copyright, 1955, by Edita S. A., Lausanne.

"Speed Was His Spur" by Dennis May, reprinted from *Road & Track*, by permission of the publisher, John Bond. Copyright, 1951, by Enthusiasts' Publications, Inc.

"The Short, Unhappy Life of the Monzetta" by Charles Beaumont, reprinted from *Sports Cars Illustrated* by permission of the author. Copyright, 1959, by Ziff-Davis Publishing Co.

"Ascari's Last Curve" by John Fitch, reprinted from *The Atlantic Monthly* by permission of the author. Copyright, 1957, by Atlantic Monthly, Inc.

"Speed at Daytona Beach" by Peter Lyon, reprinted from *Holiday Magazine* by permission of the author and of his agent, Ashley-Steiner-Famous Artists, Inc. Copyright, 1960, by Holiday Magazine.

"Racing Is a Vice" by Alfonso De Portago, reprinted from *Sports Illustrated* (May 13, 1957, issue) by permission of Sports Illustrated, Time, Inc. Copyright, 1957, by Time, Inc.

"Postscript: Death at Guidizzolo" (an excerpt from "Tragedy at the Mille Miglia") by William Rospigliosi, reprinted from *Sports Illustrated* (May 20, 1957, issue) by special permission of Sports Illustrated, Time, Inc. Copyright, 1957, by Time, Inc.

"Gentle Jimmy" by John Tomerlin reprinted from *Sports Car Graphic* by permission of the author. Copyright, 1962, by Petersen Publishing Co.

"Mickey Thompson: Recordbreaker" by Wayne Thoms, reprinted from *Motor Trend* by permission of the author. Copyright, 1962, by Petersen Publishing Co.

"Go, Man, Go!" by Randall Jarrell, reprinted from *Mademoiselle* by permission of the author. Copyright, 1957, by Randall Jarrell.

Bantam Books are published by Bantam Books, Inc. Its trade-mark, consisting of the words "Bantam Books" and the portrayal of a bantam, is registered in the United States Patent Office and in other countries. Marca Registrada. Printed in the United States of America. Bantam Books, Inc., 271 Madison Ave., New York 16, N. Y.

CONTENTS

INTRODUCTION

When engines roar on the circuits of the world, excitement begins. Our book is an honest attempt to convey this excitement to the reader, be he novice or veteran, enthusiast or casual browser. Here he will find dramatic material on the great drivers, great cars, and great circuits, written by the stars of the automotive field.

In assembling this material, ranging from Monte Carlo to Indianapolis, from Tazio Nuvolari to Bill Vukovich, from huge record cars to rally-equipped Volkswagens, we have made this as modern and up-to-date a book as possible—yet, in large part, it is a nostalgic volume. We did not *aim* for nostalgia; it simply became a legitimate part of our book. Why? Because of one basic fact which cannot be ignored or bypassed: the Brutes are gone.

We think of a big 250F Maserati on the Nürburgring, roaring a full-throated challenge to its rivals, sliding its massive, riveted bullet tail around the tight curves, a giant among giants; we think of a bright crimson side-tank Lancia-Ferrari at Monaco, slamming its thunder through the batwing-black Monte Carlo tunnel, leading a fierce pack; we think of a Mercedes 300 SLR, bombing along the Mulsanne straight at Le Mans in full song. . . .

But all this is no more. The "day of the Brute" is past, gone, vanished—and, in its place, we have the tiny, toy-like BRM, the fragile Lotus, the cobbled-together (at this writing) ATS. Even the legendary, always-savage Ferrari seems, in its current, economical, rear-engined version, only a shadow of its former self. Of course, the change was inevitable; the brutes had to die. Progress demanded it. But we were at Monte Carlo in 1960, and the car we remember was not the sleek little round-the-corner-on-rails Lotus driven to victory by Stirling Moss, but rather the bouncing, growling, sliding, front-engined Ferrari manhandled by Phil Hill to an awesome third overall. Along with many others who thrilled to the mighty, massive racing cars of yesterday, we feel that the sport has lost much of its magic, that progress has robbed us of the great drama—the pride and majesty of a really fierce machine, battling others equally as fierce and majestic.

We sing also of the drivers, who rode their fearsome steeds to a special kind of glory, in a special kind of way. The flamboyant ones, the compulsive ones, the colorful ones. A few are left, but only a few. And of that handful, most seem almost embarrassed at their survival. Farina, Fangio, Moss—they all live, but they no longer race. They stand by, bemused, as the crisp, impeccable, nearly invisible and nearly nameless drivers of this age conduct their little power toys with precision, and at speeds never attained by the great *piloto*s of the past.

Don't get us wrong. Road racing is still an immensely exciting sport, a spectacle to remember. Today, it is simply a *different* kind of excitement, a spectacle less spectacular. It is safer—and this we heartily applaud—but that special flair is missing.

In this collection, the brutes are celebrated—from the very early days of Racing's Roaring Age to the sunset period when the front-engined beasts were soon to disappear from our ken. We loved them; we mourn them. And, here, we celebrate them.

In *When Engines Roar* we are with Ascari on his "last curve"; we are with Sir Malcolm Campbell at Pendine Sands, ready to blast the land speed record with the mammoth Bluebird; we take a fond, backward glance at Model Ts and Marmons with John Steinbeck; we compare the glittering, gaudy careers of Fangio and Nuvolari with Ken Purdy; we are at Daytona for the noise and glamor of Speed Week; we slam and pitch over the outback country of Australia on the mad Redex Trail; we gun past the grandstands at Indianapolis with Bill Vukovich, as "Indy's Iron Man" tries desperately for the hat trick, three wins in a row at the Brickyard; we roar over a thousand-mile ribbon of twisting Italian road at suicidal speeds with Stirling Moss in the 1955 Mille Miglia; we share the dark fate of the doomed Frenchman, Levegh, as he precipitates motor racing's greatest tragedy at Le Mans; we whip under the checker in 1921, winning the French Grand Prix with Jimmy Murphy, the first American ever to achieve this singular honor.

All these moments and many others are vividly relived in these pages. But while motor racing will continue to thrill millions with its own unique brand of excitement, the fabled era of brute power, of cumbersome machines sliding the turns in ragged thunder, is behind us now.

We repeat: the brutes are gone. But for a few shining hours their engines roar again in these pages. We think you'll agree that the music is very sweet indeed.

William F. Nolan
Charles Beaumont

THE WORLD'S FINEST—FANGIO OR NUVOLARI?

by Ken W. Purdy

Two more different personalities could scarcely be imagined than Tazio Nuvolari and Juan Manuel Fangio. The former, a totally-committed competitor, lived only for racing; the latter, a seemingly phlegmatic, disinterested businessman, happened to race fast automobiles. But an examination of the two men, as shown by Ken Purdy's probing article, reveals that the differences are superficial. No man devotes his adult life to the world's most dangerous sport, and lives through the experience, without the characteristics of both these champions. Both were committed, each in his own way, both touched compulsively by the fire of genius. Both were great. As to who was the greater, it is a question one can never truly answer. Who was the greatest lover of all time, the greatest author, the greatest torero? Yet it is grand fun to speculate—as Ken Purdy does here.

When Juan Manuel Fangio won the 19th Grand Prix of Germany at the Nürburgring in August, of 1957, breaking the lap record *ten times* to come home 3.6 seconds ahead of Mike Hawthorn after 312 miles of racing, most of the experts present slumped back into their seats and told themselves that they had seen the Old Man in the best performance of his life, and one of the best performances of all time. The correspondent of *The Motor* went all the way. He said that Fangio's had been "the most breathtaking exhibition of driving since Nuvolari."

It had to come eventually, a citation of the fabulous Argentinian as the peer of the Italian who has until now been universally regarded as the greatest automobile driver who ever held a wheel in his hands. (The more chauvinistic Italians are quick to argue that Fangio really belongs to them: he is only a first-generation Argentinian and his parents were born in Italy.) Now that Fangio has retired perhaps the question can be settled, or as nearly settled as such comparisons ever are.

5

If the 1957 Grand Prix of Germany was in fact Fangio's greatest race the comparison benefits because one of Nuvolari's major triumphs was on the Nürburgring, three decades ago, in 1935. Unlike Fangio, Nuvolari came to the Ring that year an underdog.

On form, Fangio figured to win the Nürburgring in 1957. He had won it three times in the past, and three times in succession at that. He held the lap record for the 17.6-mile course of steep grades and mean curves at 9 minutes 41.6 seconds, 87.74 miles per hour, and he broke it on the first day of practice at 9 minutes 25.6 seconds, an average of 90.29 miles per hour. Before the race was over he had broken it eight times more, pounding it down to 9.17.4 or almost 92 miles an hour. He started on the pole, carrying a half-tank of fuel, and ran behind Hawthorn and Collins until the third lap, when he took over. He led until the 12th lap, when he stopped to pick up two new rear tires and another half-tank of fuel. (Hawthorn and Collins had started with full tanks, did not have to re-fuel.) The pit stop cost him 56 seconds and put him 33 seconds behind the leader, Hawthorn, on the 13th lap. He spent one lap apparently trying to lull the two Ferrari drivers into a false security, dropping three seconds further behind to do it. Then he opened the tap and began closing on them; 32 seconds, 25, 20, 13, 3 seconds. Hawthorn was still leading, Collins second. On the last lap Fangio passed Collins, was re-passed, took him again, caught Hawthorn and won going away to post an average speed of 88.79, faster than his 1956 record lap. Fangio's performance was astounding for sheer speed and virtuosity, and memorable, too, for coolness and strategy (the sacrifice of a pit-stop for the early lightness of a half-load of fuel, the craft that half-convinced the Ferrari team, for a precious few minutes, that his Lap 12 stop had ended his chance of winning). It was a perfect race, and Fangio ran it as always: cold, unruffled, thinking miles and minutes ahead, surprised never. Those who have called it his greatest race are probably right.

When Tazio Nuvolari came to the Nürburgring in 1935 for what was to be *his* greatest race, the role laid out for him was strictly that of spear-carrier. Nobody conceded him a chance. In the first place, his right leg and foot were in plaster of paris, and no one believed that even Nuvolari could drive, much less win on one of the toughest brake-and-accelerate courses ever laid out with a lump of stone on his business foot. (With the *brio* that was characteristic of him, and that contrasts so strongly with Fangio's modesty, Nuvolari told a friend that he couldn't care less, he intended just to lay the thing on the go-pedal and leave it there.)

Secondly, Nuvolari was mounted on an ancient car that was demonstrably slower than the machinery being used by the favorites: two full teams of Auto-Unions and Mercedes-Benz man-eaters, nine of them in all. He was driving a P-3 Alfa that was, compared with the German single-seaters of the time, a technological orphan. The P-3 in its original form was a 2.6-liter straight-eight carrying two blowers, and in 1932 and 1933 it had been a world-beater. It had 190 horsepower and could do 140 miles an hour. It was very light, due in part to the famous double drive-shaft which split the power at the gear-box and took it to bevel gears at each rear wheel. The car Nuvolari drove at the Nürburgring had a 3.8-liter engine and at 305 horsepower was giving away 125 to the 25W Mercedes-Benz, at 430, and 70 bhp to the Auto-Unions. It was generally agreed among experts on the ground that Nuvolari's P-3 was about 15 miles an hour slower than the 175 mph 25W Mercedes and 20 miles under the B-type Auto-Union, which would do 180.

When the flag fell the torque of the 4-liter and 4.5-liter Germans told and Nuvolari was nowhere. He was 6th going into the sixth lap and everyone expected him to run there, lending a little color to the proceedings, and finish out of the money. But in the 7th lap the little 43-year-old Italian began to demonstrate that he had been conning the opposition. He pulled the handle and blew off a couple of cars and then took the great Bernd Rosemeyer, destined to be the best of the Auto-Union pilots. He set out after the next in line, Louis Chiron, lying 3rd, and by the 10th lap he had taken Chiron and Brauchitsch and was the biggest thing in Caracciola's rear-view mirrors. He took Caracciola in that lap and was leading the race when he went in for fuel. He expected to hold the lead, since everybody else had to re-fuel, too, but while the Germans did it in as little as 47 seconds, Nuvolari's pit took 2 minutes 14 seconds. (A mighty-muscled Alfa mechanic, in ecstasy over "Nivola's" performance, twisted the handle off the pump, and the rest had to be done with cans, while Nuvolari, never a model of calm, screamed and rent his garments.)

He came out of the pit lying fifth, faced with the tiresome necessity of beating the Germans all over again. There was no reason to suppose that he could do it. Their cars were faster, and they knew now what they were dealing with. But Nuvolari, on his good days, could always make a car go faster than it could go, and he took Caracciola, Rosemeyer and Faglioli again, and he did it in one lap. Brauchitsch was leading, and the good gray Neubauer was on the edge of the track holding up GO signs, whiskey-bottles and according to some possibly biased observers, a medium-caliber sporting rifle significant of the fate that awaited the red-headed Mercedes pilot if he didn't get his foot well and truly into it. Brauchitsch, not always a model of obedience, did as he was told and broke the lap record. But he couldn't keep it up, and Nuvolari began to make a steady 16 seconds a lap on him. Brauchitsch's tires were wearing visibly as a result of the flogging he was giving them, and he knew that to get home in one piece he ought to stroke it a little. Neither Neubauer, red-eyed with fury, nor Nuvolari, taking every corner in an impossible drift, would cooperate, however, and so he kept on spinning them until, in the last lap, one let go and Nuvolari blasted past him to win. Expert consensus was that he had beaten Brauchitsch twice: given a normal refuelling stop he'd have beaten him without the blown tire, and as it was he beat him by forcing him to over-extend his car. The question that can never be answered, though, is this: How did he get the old P-3 within striking distance of *any* of the nine German cars, even once?

Since it has to be conceded that the 250F Maserati Fangio used at the Nürburgring was at least as good a machine as the Ferraris he beat with it, it doesn't seem to me that he proved himself a greater driver than Nuvolari in August of '57. Nuvolari's fastest lap speed in 1935 was 79.3 and Fangio's, on a surface probably about as good—it was new when Nuvolari ran on it and it has been partially re-surfaced since—was 91.4. The 12.1 difference is logical in the light of 22 years of technological evolution.

Since there were only national championships to be won in Nuvolari's time, no world title, it is impossible to place him against Fangio's five world championships. And since the major races are not the same today as they were 20 years ago, a hypothetical standard cannot be established. In 1935, when Nuvolari was at the top of his form, counting Grand Prix races alone, he had six first places, a second and a third, which would give him, by today's point system, a total of 64. A little more than half that many would have been enough to win in '57, but on the other hand Fangio won eight races that year, not six. In 1933 Nuvolari was first ten times, and his wins that year included both Le Mans and the Mille Miglia. His life-time record shows only 16 seconds, 9 thirds. As a rule, he either won or broke up the car. Here again he is at the opposite pole from Fangio, who was almost never forced out of a race by over-stressed machinery. Fangio, who began life as a mechanic, has an uncanny perception of the strain an engine will accept, and no one since Rudi Caracciola has been easier on his mounts.

Through '57, Fangio ran in 95 G. P. races and won 41 of them. He placed second 20 times and 3rd twice.

Nuvolari's record is 172 races, 64 wins. Again, the comparison is not altogether valid because when Nuvolari, after a period of bicycle and motorcycle racing, entered his first car race on May 22nd, 1921, it was the Circuito del Garda, an established road-course. Fangio's early races were hairy, hell-for-leather things in the Argentine hot-rod category, *Mecanica National,* mechanics' races run in home-assembled *bolides,* most of which were unsanitary in the extreme. Fangio ran "specials" powered by everything but trained mice. He even had a Rickenbacker going for him at one time. But the *Mecanica National* races, if they were primitive affairs by European standards, made brutally efficient training events, and Fangio's great feeling for machinery undoubtedly came from the necessity of holding a tired Chevrolet together over hundreds of miles of dusty pampas and switch-back mountain roads. He ran in 32 of these races. He won his first *Mecanica National* race in 1940, a Buenos Aires-Lima-Buenos Aires go-round (distance 5932 miles) in a Chevrolet. After that, it was the old story: he began to be offered the wheel on good cars, and when the Argentine government sent a team abroad for the 1949 season Fangio won six out of ten events. Two years later he was champion of the world. He competed for 22 years; Nuvolari drove his last race in 1950, 29 years after the first.

There seems small point in carrying the factual comparison much farther than that, although it could be done. Perhaps if we fed into an IBM machine the total number of miles each driver ran in his competitive life-time, setting Nuvolari's motorcycle races against Fangio's *Mecanica National* events, added the average speeds weighted for barometric pressure and track temperature, plus Pomeroy's Formula for annual increase, with c.c. of engine capacity with allowance for blowing, we might arrive at a more nearly exact analysis. But in fact the intangibles are more interesting.

Both were kind, gentle, considerate men off the circuit. S. C. Davis of *The Autocar* said of Nuvolari, "I think that the thing we shall remember most of that gallant little man will be his essential friendliness . . . there was something about him that attracted one immediately." Even Achille Varzi, Nuvolari's bitterest rival, always referred to Nuvolari in his absence as "Il Maestro." Legend to the contrary, Nuvolari was not a rough or dirty competitor. He would not give an inch of his ground to his best friend, but he wouldn't take what wasn't his, either. He knew the rules, though, and he beat Varzi out of a Mille Miglia, one of the three times he won that race, by driving flatout for 50 miles without a light showing, until he had come up to Varzi, who was stroking, a sure winner, then switching on and passing him. As for Fangio he was very probably the best-liked G.P. driver of his time. Mild, calm, amused and amusing, he made no enemies in his profession and I at least have never heard a harsh word said about him. And—here again the difference—he maintained this demeanor on the circuit to a greater extent than Nuvolari ever did. Nuvolari, with his foot in it, was pretty much all business. He usually left the social amenities in his pit. Drivers running into a corner with the great Mantuan did not expect to be waved ahead, and they weren't; if they cut him off, inadvertently or otherwise, they knew they would be informed of his displeasure promptly via an extensive pantomimic vocabulary. Fangio was more than polite, he was courtly. He never forgot a favor or a kindness granted him by another driver, and to be sure that the fellow had noted his gesture of appreciation, he was likely to repeat it the next time he lapped him. He knew where his friends were on the circuit, and he let them see that he knew. In 1956, at Sebring, Diana Bartley walked around the whole 5.2-mile circuit to take photographs. Fangio kept track of her progress and waved to her on every lap.

Considerable nonsense has been retailed down the years by writers discoursing on drivers' varying "styles." It is amusing to see photographs of three drivers placed side-by-side under a sober caption urging the reader to note the difference in style. Usually the differences are so minute as to be nearly invisible: perhaps one driver's elbow is bent at ten degrees to 15 for his colleague, and that's about it. However, a valid comparison is possible between Fangio and

10

Nuvolari. Fangio sat as relaxed as a plate of *pasta*, every muscle apparently limp. He had his back well into the upholstery, his arms nearly straight out in a modification of the manner first used by Dr. Farina and carried to its extreme by Stirling Moss. He indulged in no dramatics. If he wanted to check the condition of the rear tires, he did not do it in front of the main grandstand at 160 miles per hour. He looked straight ahead. Except in the mad rush for the first corner after the start, you somehow did not often see Fangio in an elbow-to-elbow dust-up with other drivers.

Nuvolari was a dramatist, and he played the role of racing driver to the hilt. He sat straight up, his shoulders often not touching the seat-back at all, his body close to the wheel, his elbows bent. He bounced in the seat. He shouted, he smiled at other drivers, or glared at them in anger, or looked through them in haughty indifference. Sometimes, flying down a straight with the gas-pedal flattened on the floor, he would hark back to his country boyhood and beat on the side of the car as if it were a laggard horse. He threw himself from side to side in the cockpit. He seemed to use the wheel more than other drivers of his day, moved it oftener and through greater arcs, perhaps because his attack in corners was so radical, his drifts more frequent and sharper than others. Nuvolari's style was original with him, and came about, he said, because he found that at 135 pounds he did not have sufficient strength to horse the big cars of the time around. He found it simpler to let them follow the course they wanted to take, that is, to drift out, and to control them with throttle and steering adjustments, guided by his incredible sense of balance. Some authorities have credited Nuvolari with originating the four-wheel drift. Undoubtedly it had been used before him; but just as surely Nuvolari did develop and perfect it as a cornering technique and thereby he profoundly influenced every driver who came after him.

Nuvolari drove on the roads with almost as much dash as he used on the circuits. He drove fast, and if he had an interested passenger, he might deliver an illustrated lecture on the subject of drifting, or the use of bumps and ridges in the roadway. These lectures could be very stimulating, even if delivered in something no hairier than a Fiat *Topolino,* and his passengers were apt to remember them.

A LIFE profile depicted Fangio as a veritable model driver who meticulously obeys every rule in the book, and particularly never breaks the speed limit. It's true that he is not really a wild man on the road, but, like Nuvolari and nearly all big-time drivers, he usually does hurry.

A few years ago, he came around a corner at about 85 to find two cars abreast on the road. He took to the fields, went around a big tree and came back on the road, never, of course, having touched the brake. A ride with Fangio is stimulating, too—as an example of intelligence applied to the business of staying alive. Actually Fangio does not care for road-driving. He loathed the Mille Miglia, and although he finished second the year Moss won, he finally refused to run in it at all. His reason, cited by Portago, was widely quoted: "No one with a conscience can run fast in the Mille Miglia."

Fangio could be a bold pilot when he felt it was warranted, as when he broke up a car at Monaco, bouncing it off telephone poles and building corners trying to catch Stirling Moss, but for the most part he abhorred risk and wanted the percentage on his side. Nuvolari would accept ridiculous hazards—and he had the scars to prove it. He was said to have broken every bone in his body at least once and 17 times hospital bulletins listed him as "serious" or "critical." (The 18th time, it stuck.) Fangio was badly hurt only once: He flipped a Maserati at Monza in 1952, severely injuring his back. He refused to run in the abortive "500" race at Monza, on the ground that it was too dangerous, a stand in which he was joined by most of the European G.P. drivers. It was just plainly a bad business proposition.

Fangio won every important G.P. circuit race in the world at least once, excepting Indianapolis. It is the only big one the Old Man never ran in. Nuvolari did run in a *monoposto* G.P. event in America, the Vanderbilt Cup of 1936, which he won, blowing off the likes of Wilbur Shaw and Mauri Rose, who, to be fair, were pushing equipment entirely unsuited to the job at hand.

Mere money can no longer tempt Fangio. He is at least once a millionaire. Nuvolari, too, was well-off when he died, although not as wealthy as the Argentinian. Both have been careful spenders and good bookkeepers, living as they drove, looking ahead. Fangio never drove on a G.P. circuit that he did not know as well as he knew his own driveway at home, and Nuvolari, in practice, could often be seen trying the shoulder at full bore, to find out what it would be like to be forced off. In competition he often seemed to be driving as if he didn't know what was around the next corner and didn't care, but if there was a stone as big as a hen's egg sticking out of the tar anywhere on the circuit Nuvolari knew about it.

The longer one pursues the matter the harder it is to decide whether one of these men was abler than the other. Both have been conceded to be kindly, quiet beings in whom a competitive urge amounting almost to a killer-instinct burned hot. Mike Hawthorn and Peter Collins were tough drivers, but when Fangio moved out to take them at the Nürburgring they were taken and they stayed taken. Nuvolari once told a rival, "I can beat you on anything, including bicycles." They borrowed bikes and adjourned to Monza. Nuvolari won.

Fangio won more races on percentage, but he did not have the unearthly ability to beat faster cars that Nuvolari knew, as at the Nürburgring and in the 1947 Mille Miglia, when he placed 2nd overall, and very nearly won, in *an 1,100 cc. Cisitalia*. Fangio compressed his career into a shorter span, but Nuvolari's dedication was deeper: he raced until he was so sick and so old that he had to be lifted out of the cars.

Overall, today, I think Nuvolari remains what everyone has called him for 20 years: the greatest racing driver who ever lived, and Fangio stands next, very close to him.

INDY'S IRON MAN

by Frank Anmar

Race drivers defy categorization. It is popularly held that sports car drivers are all well-dressed playboys, sprint and midget-car drivers a group of oily-fingered cretins, stock car drivers colorful roughnecks, Grand Prix drivers serious businessmen. Of Indianapolis drivers, what could possibly be said except that they are of that strange breed who will do anything, even drive around and around at 150 mph for 500 miles for the big money prize? The truth is that the sport, or business, was created by individuals for individuals. College professors race Go-Karts, while semi-illiterates may be found in Sports Ferraris. To some degree, Bill Vukovich might have been responsible for the mass opinion regarding Indy drivers: rough, fearless, insensitive, he was maniacally devoted to his job. But this simple explanation is inadequate, as this profile shows us.

American automobile racing, since its inception as a professional sport some six decades ago at the century's turn, has spawned many rugged individuals. From the tank-town dirt ovals to the fabled main arena at Indianapolis, from stock cars and midgets to the high-powered, razor-tuned Brickyard bombs, the sport has developed a hardy breed whose home is a cramped cockpit smelling of hot oil and dust and raw exhaust fumes and whose goal is a checkered cloth.

The man they called "Vukie" was of this breed, and no driver in the business was tougher or more determined to be first than was this dark-haired, hard-muscled, five-foot-nine-inch, 160 pound bundle of racing dynamite.

"Man, but ole Vukie was a mean chauffeur," said the late Walt Faulkner, a close friend to Vukovich for many years. "If he couldn't pass you, he'd run over you. I remember the first midget race I ran with him. This was on a quarter-mile track, and I was in between Vukie and a guy named Pyser. On our warm-up lap, Vuk banged his wheels against mine just to let me know what to expect. Well, I rooted him right back to show him I was no dummy. As we got the flag, Vukie banged his wheels into me again. This slapped me up against Pyser, who kissed the wall. Vukie and I tore up the backstretch and I tried to get around him coming out of the next turn, but he was having none of that. He just bashed me hard into the fence and went on to win."

During the five-day, 2,000-mile *Carrera Pan-Americana* (in 1954) Vukovich started 15th, running in the Heavy Stock class with a Lincoln. By the end of the first day he had blasted into second behind Ray Crawford, averaging better than 132 mph over abrasive tar-and-gravel straightaways and twisting Mexican roads. On the second leg of the contest, ignoring navigator Vern Houle's nervous instructions as to maximum speed for upcoming turns, Vukie lost control in the mountains. As their big machine plunged off a 50-foot cliff, Vukovich turned in disgust to his bug-eyed passenger: "Okay, Vern, *you* drive!" (The Lincoln rolled several times and was totally demolished. Houle was uninjured; Vukie broke a vertebra in his neck.)

"Vukie crashed plenty," admitted Faulkner. "He scarred his hands up, broke his shoulders, smashed his ribs. On one track he went through the fence *three* times in exactly the same place. Once he told me, 'I'm gonna quit this racket. Costs me too damn much for crash helmets.' That was Vuk!"

In 1952, at Indianapolis for his second try on the bricks, he slammed into a concrete wall on the southwest corner in lap 191, losing a clear lead he had gained over the field. Back at the pits, tears of frustration and anger in his eyes, he paced back and forth, slapping his hands together. "What a crummy, lousy break," he groaned. "I knew the steering was going—but we almost had it in the bag so I stayed on it. Then—zowey! What a stinking break!"

In 1953 he won the 500-mile classic. In 1954 he won again. In 1955 he was leading comfortably, dominating the big oval and well on the way to a third victory, when three cars spun violently in front of him. Vukie turned right to avoid the tangle and died in the wreckage of his Hopkins Special.

William Vukovich was born in Alameda, California, in 1919. Two years later his family moved to Sanger, a small farming community just southeast of Fresno. There the boy performed routine chores with his two elder brothers, Eli and Mike, on the modest family ranch and vineyard.

When he was 13, his father died, and Vukie abruptly

terminated all formal education to join Eli in a variety of back-breaking jobs. "We pruned trees, tilled fields, picked cotton and drove trucks," recalled Eli, "and we took turns paying the grocery bill."

Vukie saw his first race when he was 14. It was a roadster meet, and he never forgot that afternoon of heat and noise and fast cars. "Some day," he told Eli, "I'll be faster than *any* of 'em."

Four years passed, with Vukie haunting the local tracks and garages. His mother had died in the meantime, and with no family ties to bind him to steady employment he became wholly immersed in speed. Late in 1937, the boy finally took to the dirt in a souped-up Chevrolet after he had convinced its owner, Fred Gerhard, that he could handle the bellowing beast in competition. Vukie placed well up in this initial event, winning the third time out.

During the following season he got a chance at a midget, and promptly flipped the car, breaking three ribs and a collar bone. But he was soon back in the cockpit—often competing on the same tracks with Eli, who had also taken up the hazardous profession.

"Don't ever tangle with me," Vukie calmly told his brother, "because when we're out on that track you're just another chauffeur I gotta beat."

Vukovich couldn't stand to have Eli finish ahead of him, according to the third brother, Mike, who sometimes acted as mechanic for the other boys. He recalled one event in which Vukie lost a wheel as he was passing the pit area. Mike rushed out to get it off the track, and this action annoyed Vukie. "Now, why the devil didn't you leave the lousy wheel out there? Eli might have hit the thing on the next lap."

During this '38-'39 period, the three brothers rode the "hamburger trail," following the season from track to track in an old Ford, pulling a battered trailer on which they slept between races.

"We put our necks on the line for pork and bean money," Eli said, "and drove in over a dozen races each week, clearing maybe forty bucks when we were lucky and ending up on our heads when we weren't. But it was kicks, and we loved every dumb minute of it."

By 1940 Vukovich had forged well ahead of his racing brother, and was beginning to earn a reputation on the West Coast. They called him "The Mad Russian" since he drove as though brakes had never been invented—"I just slide high and let the mud slow me down." The nickname persisted, although Vukie was of Slavic, not Russian, descent.

"I wish you guys would at least spell my name right," he once told a group of newsmen. "When my family came over here from Yugoslavia the name was Vucurovitch, and they went to a lot of trouble to change it to Vukovich, just for characters like you."

During the war years Vukie joined a mobile repair unit, servicing trucks and tanks, and by 1945, when the war ended, he had acquired a wife, Esther, and his own "washing machine." This was a 700-pound midget racer, powered by a two-cylinder water-cooled Drake engine which Vukie had painstakingly rebuilt.

"With this little jewel," he told his wife, "I'm going out and show all those other chauffeurs my dust!"

Vukie did just that, capturing the URA Pacific Coast midget championship in '45 and '46, blazing to victory again and again in the face of superior equipment. His two-cylinder was underpowered compared to the newer Offys and V8s, yet he consistently beat faster cars—so much so that the fans grew tired of seeing his red charger (which he dubbed "Old Ironsides") lead the way to the checker. The crowd wanted a new champ, and Vukie became the man to beat.

"These jokers want to make a villain outa me," Vukovich confided to a friend. "So, fine, I'll make a pretty good villain."

But the villain and Old Ironsides continued to win—at Fresno, Sacramento, Angels Camp, Bakersfield, Tulare, Modesto. And although he was sometimes loudly booed by the fans he was actually a popular prime attraction, adding a special color and excitement to any race he drove.

Like a coin, Vukie had two sides. Off the dirt, he was a gentle family man whose devotion never wavered, and was a favorite among his fellow drivers. His bluff tone disguised a basic shyness and most of his explosive remarks were delivered strictly for effect.

He smashed up frequently in those days, but he coolly figured such incidents as "part of the game when you play for keeps." He wouldn't slow down.

At Tulare he demolished the faithful Drake-engined midget when a broken radius rod flipped the red car skyward. After this crash Esther begged him to retire. Instead he bought a faster offy-powered machine and stormed his way to the 1950 AAA National Championship.

Having reached the pinnacle of success in the small bombs, he now tackled the big ones with the same fierce energy, working his way up to a ride at Indianapolis.

In 1951 Pete Salemi, of Cleveland, offered Vukie a chance to hit the bricks in his Central Excavating Special. Vukovich qualified the car in the seventh row, but expressed a strong hunch that he would not finish.

"This sled will last about 30 laps and then fall apart," he declared.

At 15 laps he was running among the top 10, but his unhappy prediction was borne out on lap 29, when he was forced from the contest with an oil leak.

"This Indy race is a cinch," he commented. "I should have been here years ago."

Vukie was in his element at the Brickyard, and a year later he led the event for 185 laps before "kissing the wall" with steering failure.

"Next year I'll show these hot dogs the way home," he told Esther, squeezing a hard rubber ball in his right hand as he talked. This was part of the Vukovich training plan, designed to strengthen his hand muscles. He also favored a mile run each morning ("for the legs") and he didn't smoke ("it gets you in the lungs").

It was during this time that Vukie turned from midgets to devote his full attention to the larger cars. He did well the following season, but his thoughts were always on Indianapolis. In Vukie's mind the 500 represented the greatest challenge any driver could meet, and winning it became an obsession.

It was during the 1953 Brickyard classic that Vukovich came to be known as "Indy's Iron Man." He began by qualifying his Keck Fuel Injection Special in hair-raising fashion: on his third timed lap a light rain began to drizzle down from the dark sky, and it was assumed he would not attempt another full-throttle tour of the big oval under these dangerous conditions. But Vukie knew he might well lose the pole slot if he backed off. Foot jammed down on the accelerator, he flashed by for a staggering four-lap average of 138.382—a new record. As the sky opened, drenching the track surface, his big car fishtailed violently, but he made the pits without incident. Vukie had the pole.

On race day the weather reversed itself, the temperature quickly climbing into the 90s. One by one, cars dropped out, or switched drivers. The big oval was a sun-blazed inferno. Of the 33-car field, only Vukovich and four others drove the full 500 miles without relief at the wheel.

Vukie had indeed led the "hot dogs" home. He won in grand style, grossing a fantastic $89,496 for the blistering run. His share of the money (well over $35,000) allowed him to retire and spend the year in Fresno with his family, which now included a boy, Bill, Jr., and a daughter, Marlene.

His rough-edged sense of humor asserted itself as the date of the 1954 500-miler approached. At the garage where his special was being prepared he tacked up a photo of Old Ironsides, telling the crew: "When the going gets too rough for you butchers, just take a look at *this* hunk of iron."

As a result of the '54 qualifying runs, Vukie found himself "buried" in 19th position. None of the winners in the past seven races at Indy had started farther back than seventh, and pre-race betting did not favor the Fresno leadfoot.

"Nuts," snapped Vukovich, when he heard the odds. "A guy can win from *any* position. Before this clambake is very old I'll be up there in front, showing these dummies my tailpipe. Just watch me."

And everyone did. Battling his way through the roaring field, he sliced past car after car as the laps ticked away. By the 92nd tour he was where he'd vowed to be, in the lead. And this is where he stayed, winning his second victory on the bricks. (In his pocket Vukie carried a scrawled note from his small son: "Dear Daddy—smoke those hot dogs off the track!")

When they asked him how he'd done it, Vukie snorted: "Anybody, and that includes my grandmother, can drive down these big straightaways. But if you want those fat lap times, you've got to punch it on the turns. So I punch it."

Actually, the Vukovich method included out-braking his opponents into the turns, passing without regard to turn or straightaway, changing his line if need be to get around another car—a speedway technique as unorthodox, yet as effective, as the road technique of Tazio Nuvolari.

Vukie had now reached the same racing pinnacle with the big cars that he had attained in the midgets, and there seemed no real point in continuing. He had invested in a pair of gas stations in Fresno and put aside a trust fund for his children, in addition to other business ventures. The time seemed ideal to hang up the helmet.

"Why not call it quits, honey?" his wife asked him. "What more *is* there?"

"The hat trick," replied Vukie, his voice low and intense. "Winning Indy three times in a row. Nobody's done it yet, but I think I can be the slob to pull it off."

Esther didn't argue; she knew her husband too well for that. In 1955 Vukie would return to Indianapolis.

Veteran Troy Ruttman, commenting on Vukie's desire to become the first three-time winner, believed he could pull it off. "He can do it. He's got just what it takes—determination, hustle, brains. With Vuk it's always fight, fight. He'll never give up."

Vukovich arrived early for the '55 qualifying runs, circling the big speedway again and again in practice.

His buddy, Walt Faulkner, was puzzled. "I watched ole Vukie going round and round. He sat very still in the car, like he was thinking about something deep, using the track to iron things out. He must have gone about fifty miles like that, just holding steady at about 90. It worried me, the way he looked."

In the pits the Vukovich temper flared, and he seemed exceptionally nervous. His hunches had always paid off, and now he seemed to have a hunch there would be trouble in his try for the triple victory.

"Esther, this is crazy," he blurted out the night before the race. "What are we doing here? Let's go home."

And to fellow-driver Terry Hoyt, on race morning: "Freaks—that's what they think us chauffeurs are. And you know something? They're right."

But when the gleaming cars, row upon glittering row, were rolled out to the grid Vukie was there with his light blue 350-hp Hopkins Special. He'd made the second row with a qualifying run of 141.071—and pre-race odds favored him 7 to 1.

At 9:55 A.M. Tony Hulman issued the familiar command: "Gentlemen, start your engines."

The minute-by-minute race report tells the story . . .

10:01—The pace car pulls to the apron as the field is released with Jack McGrath taking the lead.

10:05—Bill Vukovich has charged into second, moving very fast at the end of the second lap.

10:07—A battle for the front position rages as Vukovich passes McGrath.

10:16—The Fresno champion's lead is threatened as McGrath paces him, wheel to wheel down the main straight.

10:26—On lap 25 McGrath leads Vukovich by a single car-length past the stands.

10:51—On lap 48 Vukovich has a 10-second margin on McGrath.

11:02—The Iron Man has posted a new Indianapolis track record: 125 miles at an average of 135.212 mph! With a 20-second lead his third consecutive victory seems assured. Jack McGrath is out, and the track is clear.

11:03—Disaster! Rodger Ward, streaking out of the southwest turn, loses control as an axle snaps. His car spins wildly, smashing into a bridge abutment, which severs both front wheels. Al Keller and Johnny Boyd also lose control in an attempt to miss Ward. Keller slams into Boyd, and Vukovich bullets into the melee at 140, tries to avoid the other cars by twisting to the right, strikes Boyd, is airborne, rolls end over end seven times, rams a power pole, bounces into a parked sedan, a truck, and a jeep, thrashing up once again to land upside down in flames. Gray smoke billows up from the scene of the crash.

Under the battered carcass of the Hopkins Special, William Vukovich was trapped, dead from a skull fracture before the car stopped bouncing.

It was all over for the Iron Man. Swiftly, tragically over.

Journalist Russ Catlin paid him the final tribute: "He was a strange one, that Vukie . . . but he will always be remembered . . . as great as any man who ever pulled on a racing glove."

ROSES IN THE RAIN

by William F. Nolan

Of the many appeals of motor racing, not the least is the glamour. If you were to attend only the Formula World Championship events of a single season, you would be able to partake in the pleasures of nearly a dozen romantic cities throughout the world. The most romantic, by far, is Monte Carlo, for this city is not near a circuit—it *is*, for a few days every year, a circuit. William F. Nolan, justly considered to be one of the two or three most accomplished automotive writers in the business, sings here of the beauties of that distant paradise—and of racing at its best.   C. B.

Once each year in spring, inevitable as the cool mistral which scours the blue sweep of sunblazed Mediterranean, the Gods of the Road come to Monte Carlo. To the land of the roulette wheel, the Bikini and the Barbary fig is added the jungle roar of thoroughbred automobiles as the champions of the world gather to match speed and courage in the last of the great "round the houses" continental motor races, the *Grand Prix de Monaco*.

Here, several days prior to the race itself, the crack international teams assemble: Ferrari, B.R.M., Lotus, Cooper —manned by the sport's elite from England, Sweden, Australia, New Zealand, Italy, France, Germany, Scotland and America.

Since the first race was run through the ribboning streets some 35 years ago the legendary idols of speed have all won splendid victories here: Nuvolari, Varzi, Caracciola, Farina, Fangio of Argentina and Moss of England. Because of its magnificent setting, this event at Monte Carlo—traditionally the season's Grand Prix opener—is unique in motor sport.

Since 1929, many titanic automotive battles have been waged in this tiny principality (half the size of New York's Central Park) set like a blazing jewel on a high, white limestone cliff mid-way between Nice and the Italian-French border along the rocky, scenic *Cote d'Azur*. It was here, in 1955, that Ascari's furiously-driven Lancia plunged into the harbor; here, in 1932, that Nuvolari, clad in his famed yellow sweater with its rolled sleeves, bested his fierce rival Varzi: sun-scarlet Alfa vs. sky-blue Bugatti. It was Monte Carlo, in 1936, that saw the massive, power-laden thunder-wagons of Germany duelling in the rain like savage cats for the prize: Auto-Union vs. Mercedes. The names of the great cars and their drivers quicken the heart and fire the blood, and they *all* came, eventually, to Monte Carlo . . .

We learn something of the fascinating history of Monaco itself as we await the days of speed. It is a history of blood and conquest, extending back to Henry VI, a Roman emperor who first gave Monaco to the Genoese in 1191. By 1856 the site was firmly in the domain of Prince Charles III of France, who established gaming tables for which the principality is now world famous. In 1863 François Blanc built a casino in Monte Carlo—and the incredible legends of doomed souls began to flourish.

As the rosewood roulette wheels spun away all their earthly goods, hauntingly beautiful women swallowed poison in the casino gardens, while proud men boldly leaped from the towering rocks into the blue-green depths of the Mediterranean. Counts and Grand Dukes wagered castle and mistress on the maddening caprice of the tiny, dancing ivory ball—and a host of professional gamblers came to the casino to match their "infallible" systems against the wheels.

Then, in 1929, another kind of gambler came to the lush French Riviera: the continental motor aces who coolly wagered life against death. They brought their own wheels, attached to bellowing, panther-quick racing machines. The mysterious Englishman, William Grover (who competed as "Williams") won that initial race through the streets in an immortal greyhound-lean Bugatti.

A new kind of fame had come to Monte Carlo . . .

Now the wheeled panthers are about to unleash their power; now the first practice session is about to begin . . .

Due to the severity of the circuit, only 16 cars are allowed to make up the starting field. Since perhaps two-dozen drivers are on hand, the fiercely-competitive practice session continues into the dusk as glowing neons illuminate the fashionable shops behind the pit area. Early diners at the Rampoldi drink *Bouquet de Provence* as they watch the cars cannon past—and an old prune-wrinkled man orders another beer on the quay, oblivious to the din beyond the bar.

The circuit itself is extremely tricky, snaking through Monte Carlo's streets and boulevards for a length just under two miles. It begins with a short run along the quay, fronting the harbor. An abrupt right-hand turn at the Gasworks takes the field back behind the pits on the straight along Boulevard Albert I to Sainte Devote corner, then up the steeply climbing Avenue de Monte Carlo through a brief series of Esses to Casino Corner, downhill to the pretzel-shaped Station Hairpin, with the descent ending at the turn into Boulevard Louis II, then a dip into the raven's-wing blackness of the tunnel (where only the bravest maintain full-throttle) to a fast chicane leading out along the quay again to the final, sharp left-hander onto the pit straight. This, then, is the fabled "round the houses" circuit—the last of the classic city street races, providing a test for man and machine unlike any other in Europe.

A final practice session is held on Saturday afternoon, and that night, as a moon the color of Cinzano climbs the darkening sky above Monte Carlo, team mechanics patiently make final adjustments, perfecting engines for Sunday's brutal 100-lap contest.

The heavy clamoring bells of the Church of St. Charles announce the day. By noon the streets are closed to normal traffic. Stairways and alleys are blocked by barricades; stout fencing holds back the incautious. Resembling a city under siege, Monte Carlo girds itself for motorized battle.

The competing cars roll smoothly into position on the bannered quay front, forming seven rows. The sky is overcast and sunless; a grossly-distended cloud over the *Alpes Maritimes* presages rain. The waters of the Mediterranean lap quietly against the gray, monolithic stones outside the harbor entrance. Date palms stir faintly, and the scarlet Riviera flowers burn against the cool green of the casino gardens. Multi-colored villas and apartments dot the cliffs, rising in steps like an immense layer cake above the streets.

Now the crowd gathers, jamming the grandstands along the pit straight and Casino Corner, filing slowly out onto the flowered lawns and countless iron-lace balconies overlooking the course: pert French girls in full swirling dresses, their dark hair piled high to frame cream-white faces; regal, blonde-bearded Danes; Italian girls in bright sweaters and Capri pants; sad-eyed Belgians; red-faced, mustachioed Englishmen; crewcut Americans in Bermuda shorts—and the native Monégasques, tall with pride for their small city on this Sunday of Sundays.

The circuit is silent and waiting, ringed by lion-colored straw bales over which are stretched cloth ESSO and ENERGOL signs. A band on the quay sends its brassy music into the smoke-hued sky, as Rainier III makes a rapid tour of the course at the wheel of a black Peugeot sedan. His coolly-beautiful wife is beside him, the former Grace Kelly, dressed entirely in white. She waves a gloved hand as the Prince briskly slides Casino Corner.

Track workmen are whitewashing the curbs for greater definition; an artist sets up his easel, ready to paint speed; swan-white yachts dip and weave in the harbor, stitching indigo patterns in the quiet waters. High on its jutting limestone perch, the palace of Monaco—flanked by bronze cannon—seems to bestow its royal blessing. A helicopter hovers overhead like a nervous dragonfly—as a solemn-faced jeepload of black-hatted gendarmes circulates to see that the course is clear, the jeep's flag making small handclaps in the wind of its passage.

Inside the eternal Victorian gloom of the Casino the impersonal roulette wheels still turn. The players are not concerned with the mechanized battle of steel and flesh about to be fought outside; they are only concerned in their own intense struggle with the wheel of Fortune.

Now the music dies, the crowd-voice fades to a murmur—and the drivers slide into their snug cockpits, tugging at helmet straps and goggles, their minds filled with turn and straightaway, with engine revolutions and braking points.

Sixteen engines explode into life . . . the flag drops, and the *Grand Prix de Monaco* is underway: a tide of thundering metal set in motion.

Loudspeakers blare out positions—in emotionally-charged French and clipped, calm English—as the cars boom up Avenue de Monte Carlo, the metallic howl of their straining engines echoing between the terraced buildings. Now they slide wildly round the Casino and plunge downhill toward the Station Hairpin.

This is a time of thrusting nose-to-nose duels, a time to weigh courage and skill, and each driver extends his nerve and muscle to the maximum as lead positions are savagely contested. Here the man and his machine function as a single, bright entity, not wholly flesh nor wholly steel, yet each dependent on the other. A mating of bone and chassis.

At 25 laps, or quarter-distance, the sullen sky releases its first spatter of rain. The drops sift down over Monte Carlo, staining the white deck chairs and coating the turns. The waters of the Mediterranean, home of conger-eel and giant tortoise, turn to brooding purple as umbrellas are unfurled like a host of dark flowers along the high balconies.

Drivers grimly fight to maintain traction on roads gone slick as lake ice; a Ferrari spins lazily, then throttles back into the fray.

At the half-way point the sun is ironically shining between cloud patches, but the rain continues. The streets are treacherous with their wet coating of oil and rubber; brakes begin to fade; transmissions fail; engines cease—as the Prix extracts its toll.

The race roars on.

Café au lait is sipped at sidewalk tables under candy-striped awnings; champagne glasses tinkle faintly on the terrace of the Hotel de Paris as toasts are lifted to gallant drivers no longer in the fight. The early duels are over and the pattern has been set. The final triumph is at hand.

A locomotive rumble of thunder marks the downward sweep of the checkered flag—and the great contest is officially over.

Helmet off, a wreath around his neck, one hand in the air at salute, the smiling winner takes his lap of victory to the cheers of the vast crowd. The rain sheets down, a silver torrent, as he winds out of Casino Corner. A young girl, flushed and excited, rushes forward to toss three red roses at the passing champion. The flowers fall to the rain-black roadway, scattering their soft petals along the asphalt . . .

But the ritual is not yet complete.

That evening, a festive, post-race Gala begins in the lush Empire Room of the Hotel de Paris, and it is here, under the crystal fire of the teardrop chandeliers, that the last act of the *Grand Prix de Monaco* is staged.

To a sudden silence, a single stabbing drumbeat announces the entrance of the royal couple. Princess Grace steps through the wide doorway between the tall marble statues in a gown of shimmering white, followed by her Prince and their entourage. A slow-rolling drumbeat follows them to a special table—and as they are seated waiting violins sweep gayly into *The Blue Danube*.

The Gala is as wild as the race itself; there are dancing girls weaving sensuously between red-velvet pillars, and balloons and horns and top hats made of colored paper. Princess Grace does the cha-cha-cha as the band beats out frantic rhythms.

The night wears on and the last curtain falls; the violins turn sad; the dancing is done. Now the Grand Prix circus will move on, away from Monaco to other great battles— on to Spa and Zandvoort, to Silverstone, Monza and Buenos Aires, on to the other great circuits on the continent. But when it is spring once more along the blue Mediterranean the men and the cars will return to the *Cote d'Azur*.

The Gods of the Road will come back to Monte Carlo.

JALOPIES I CURSED AND LOVED

by John Steinbeck

America's Nobel Prizewinner, John Steinbeck, is a man of many passions. His robust, tough-tender approach to life has been brilliantly set down in his books, several of which are now classics. Steinbeck has never worried about his "direction" as a creative writer; he has gone on, happily turning out novels, short stories, and essays about the things he loves. In this glowing, humorous account, Steinbeck's love for that perverse beast known as "The Automobile" is clearly demonstrated.

Recently I drove from Garrison-on-Hudson to New York on a Sunday afternoon, one unit in a creeping parade of metal, miles and miles of shiny paint and chrome inching along bumper to bumper. There were no old rust heaps, no jalopies. Every so often we passed a car pulled off the road with motor trouble, its driver and passengers waiting patiently for a tow car or a mechanic. Not one of the drivers seemed even to consider fixing the difficulty. I doubted that anyone knew what the trouble was.

On this funereal tour I began to think of old times and old cars. Understand, I don't want to go back to those old dogs. Any more than I want to go back to that old poverty. I love the fine efficient car I have. But at least I remembered. I remembered a time when you fixed your own car or you didn't go any place. I remembered cars I had owned and cursed and hated and loved.

The first car I remember in the little town where I was born was, I think, a Reo with a chain drive and a steering bar. It was owned by a veterinary who got himself a bad name in Salinas for owning it. He seemed disloyal to horses. We didn't like that car. We shouted insults at it as it splashed by on Stone Street. Then, gradually, more automobiles came into town owned by the very rich. We didn't have a car for many years. My parents never accepted the

28

time-payment plan. To them it was a debt like any other debt, and to them debt was a sin. And a car cost a lot of money all in one piece.

Now it took a long time for a car to get in a condition where I could afford it, roughly about 15 years. I had an uncle who ran a Ford agency but he didn't give free samples to his relatives. He got rich selling Fords and himself drove a Stutz Bearcat—four cylinders, 16 valves. Those were proud times when he roared up in front of our house with his cutout open, sounding like a rolling barrage. But this was dream stuff and not for us.

My first two cars were Model Ts, strange beings. They never got so beat up that you couldn't somehow make them run. The first one was a touring car. Chickens had roosted on its steering wheel and I never got their marks off. The steering wheel was cracked so that if you put any weight on it it pinched your fingers when you let up. The back seat was for tools, wire and spare tires. I still confuse that car with my first love affair. The two were inextricably involved. I had it a long time. It never saw shelter or a mechanic. I remember how it used to shudder and sigh when I cranked it and how its crank would kick back viciously. It was a mean car. It loved no one, it ran in spurts and seemed to be as much influenced by magic as by mechanics.

My second Model T was a sedan. The back seat had a high ceiling and was designed to look like a small drawing room. It had lace curtains and cut-glass vases on the sides for flowers. It needed only a coal grate and a sampler to make it a perfect Victorian living room. And sometimes it served as a boudoir. There were gray silk roller shades you could pull down to make it cozy and private. But ladylike as this car was, it had also the indestructibility of ladies. Once in the mountains I stalled in a snowstorm a quarter of a mile from my cabin; I drained the water from the radiator and abandoned the car for the winter. From my window I could see it hub-deep in the snow. For some reason now forgotten, when friends visited me, we used to shoot at that car trying not to hit the glass. At a range of a quarter of a mile with a 30–30 this was pretty hard. In the spring I dug it out. It was full of bullet holes but by some accident we had missed the gas tank. A kettle of hot water in the radiator, and that rolling parlor started right off. It ran all summer.

Model Ts created a habit pattern very difficult to break. I have told the following story to the Ford Company to prove their excellence. The cooling system of the Model T was based on the law that warm water rises and cool water sinks. It doesn't do this very fast but then Model Ts didn't run very fast. Now when a Model T sprung a radiator leak, the remedy was a handful of corn meal in the radiator. The hot water cooked the meal to mush and it plugged the leak. A little bag of meal was standard equipment in the tool kit.

In the days of my nonsensical youth there were all kinds of standard practices which were normal then but now seem just plain nuts. A friend of mine had a Model T coupé, as tall and chaste as a one-holer. It rested in a lot behind his house and after a while he became convinced that someone was stealing his gasoline. The tank was under the front seat and could ordinarily be protected by locking the doors. But this car had no locks. First he left notes on the seat begging people not to steal his gasoline and when this didn't work he rigged an elaborate trap. He was very angry, you see. He designed his snare so that if anyone opened the car door, the horn would blow and a shotgun would fire.

Now, how it happened we don't know. Perhaps a drop of water, perhaps a slight earthquake. Anyway, in the middle of the night the horn went off. My friend leaped from bed, put on a bathrobe and a hat, I don't know why, raced out the back door shouting "Got you!"—yanked open the car door and the shotgun blew his hat to bits. It was his best hat too.

Well, about this time the depression came along and only increased the complications. Gasoline was hard to come by. One of my friends, wishing to impress his date, would drive into a filling station, extend two fingers out the window, out of the girl's sight, and say, "Fill her up." Then, with two gallons in the tank he would drive grandly away. This same friend worked out a way of never buying a license, which he couldn't afford anyway. He traded his car every time a license fee was due, but he only traded it for a car with a new license. His automobiles were a little worse each time but at least they were licensed.

With the depression came an era of automotive nonsense. It was no longer possible to buy a small car cheaply. Everyone wanted the Fords and Chevrolets. On the other hand, Cadillacs and Lincolns could be had for a song. There were two reasons for this. First, the big cars cost too much to run and, second, the relief committees took a sour view of anyone with a big expensive-looking car. Here is a story somewhat in point.

A friend of mine found himself in a condition of embarrassment which was pretty general and, to him, almost permanent. An old school friend, rich and retired, was going to Europe and suggested that George live in his great house in Pebble Beach in California. He could be a kind of caretaker. It would give him shelter and he could look after the house. Now the house was completely equipped, even to a Rolls-Royce in the garage. There was everything there but food. George moved in and in a first flush of joy drove the Rolls to Monterey for an evening, exhausting the tank. During the next week he ate the dry cereals left in the kitchen and set traps for rabbits in the garden. At the end of ten days he was in a starving condition. He took to staying in bed in luxury to conserve his energy. One morning, when the pangs of hunger were eating at him, the doorbell rang. George arose weakly, stumbled across the huge drawing room, across the great hall carpeted in white, and opened the baronial door. An efficient-looking woman stood on the porch. "I'm from the Red Cross," she said, holding out a pledge card.

George gave a cry of pleasure, "Thank God you've come," he said.

It was all crazy like that. It was so long since George had eaten they had to give him weak soup for quite a while.

At this time, I had an old, four-cylinder Dodge. It was a very desirable car—12-volt battery, continental gearshift, low-compression engine, supposed to run forever. It didn't matter how much oil it pumped. It ran. But gradually I detected symptoms of demise in it. We had developed an instinct for this. The trick was to trade your car in just before it exploded. I wanted something small but that I couldn't have. For my Dodge and ten dollars I got a Marmon, a great, low, racy car with aluminum body and aluminum crankcase—a beautiful thing with a deep purring roar and a top speed of nearly a hundred miles an hour. In those days we didn't look at the car first. We inspected the rubber. No one could afford new tires. The tires on the Marmon were smooth but no fabric showed, so I bought it. And it was a beautiful car—the best I had ever owned. The only trouble was that it got about eight miles to the gallon of gasoline. We took to walking a good deal, saving gasoline for emergencies.

One day there was a disturbing click in the rear end and then a crash. Now, anyone in those days knew what had happened. A tooth had broken in the ring gear of the rear end. This makes a heartbreaking noise. A new ring gear and pinions installed would come to 95 dollars or, roughly, three times what I had paid for the whole car.

It was obviously a home job, and it went this way. With a hand jack, I raised the rear end onto concrete blocks. Then I placed the jack on blocks and raised again until finally the Marmon stuck its rear end up in the air like an anopheles mosquito. Now, it started to rain. I stretched a piece of oilcloth to make a tent. I drained the rear end, removed the covers. Heavy, black grease ran up my sleeve and into my hair. I had no special tools, only a wrench, pliers and a screw driver. Special tools were made by hammering out nails on a brick. The ring gear had sheared three teeth. The pinions seemed all right but since they must be fitted, I had to discard them. Then I walked to a wrecking yard three miles away. They had no Marmons. It took a week to find a Marmon of my vintage. There were two days of bargaining. I finally got the price down to six dollars. I had to remove the ring gear and pinions myself, but the yard generously loaned tools. This took two days. Then, with my treasures back at my house I spent several days more lying on my back fitting the new parts. The ground was muddy and a slow drip of grease on my face and arms picked up the mud and held it. I don't ever remember being dirtier or more uncomfortable. There was endless filing and fitting. Kids from as far as six blocks away gathered to give satiric advice. One of them stole my pliers, but pliers were in the public domain. I had probably stolen them in the first place. I stole some more from a neighbor. It wasn't considered theft. Finally, all was in place. Now, I had to make new gaskets out of cardboard and tighten everything all around. I put in new grease, let the rear end gently down. There was no use in trying to get myself clean—that would take weeks of scrubbing with steel wool.

Now, word got around that the job was done. There was a large and friendly delegation to see the trial run—neighbors, kids, dogs, skeptics, well-wishers, critics. A parrot next door kept saying "Nuts!" in a loud squawking voice.

I started the engine. It sounded wonderful; it always sounded wonderful. I put the car in gear and crept out to the street, shifted gears and got half a block before the rear end disintegrated with a crash like the unloading of a gravel car. Even the housing of the rear end was shattered. I don't know what I did wrong but what I did was final. I sold the Marmon as it stood for 12 dollars. The junkman from whom I had bought the ring gear hauled it away—

aluminum body, aluminum crankcase, great engine, silver gray paint job, top speed a hundred miles an hour, and pretty good rubber too. Oh, well— that's the way it was.

In those days of the depression one of the centers of social life was the used-car dealer's lot. I got to know one of these men of genius and he taught me quite a bit about this business which had become a fine art. I learned how to detect sawdust in the crankcase. If a car was really beat up, a few handfuls of sawdust made it very quiet for about five miles. All the wiles and techniques of horse-trading learned over a thousand years found their way into the used-car business. There were ways of making tires look strong and new, ways of gentling a motor so that it purred like a kitten, polishes to blind the buyer's eyes, seat covers that concealed the fact that the springs were coming through the upholstery. To watch and listen to a good used-car man was a delight, for the razzle-dazzle was triumphant. It was a dog-eat-dog contest and the customer who didn't beware was simply unfortunate. For no guarantee went beyond the curb.

My friend in the used-car business offered a free radio in every car sold for one week. Now, a customer came in who hated radios. My friend was pained at this. The customer said, "All right, how much will that car be without a radio?"

My friend wrote some figures on a pad. "Well," he said, "I can let you have it for ten dollars extra—but I don't want to make a practice of it."

And the customer cheerfully paid.

It's all different now. Everything is chrome and shiny paint. A car used to be as close and known and troublesome and dear as a wife. Now we drive about in strangers. It's more comfortable, sure, but something has been lost. I hope I never get it back.

RACING'S ROARING AGE

by Russ Catlin

The days of the great fire-belching mammoths of the road are long gone. A man with the muscles of John L. Sullivan is no longer required to control a racing car. Small, agile fellows such as the swift Scot, Jim Clark, can take the laurels today. But in the Golden Age of motor racing, when all the cars were brutes and the circuits little more than chuck holes and dust, men such as Oldfield, De-Palma, and Eddie Rickenbacker roared their way into America's heart. They were the early-day Gods of the Road, and millions paid tribute to their incredible strength and daring. Historian Russ Catlin takes us back to this fabulous time, when mighty engines roared for the giants of yesterday.

A hundred thousand necks stretched, two hundred thousand eyes focused on the distant speck emerging from a dust cloud far out on Fon du Lac road. "Car coming" echoed from the crowd, and each mind asked the same question. "Is it DePalma in the grey Mercedes, or Hughes in the red Mercer?"

A few minutes before, this pair had flashed down the dusty, rutted road to start the last lap of the eighth Vanderbilt Cup race, 1912. For four hours the popular Italian and tragic little Englishman had battled for victory in the most famous of all speed contests. The end was in sight. The pair had outdistanced the rest of the field in a race that was averaging nearly 70 mph over impossible roads.

There was more than just sporting drama being re-enacted. A life was at stake. DePalma's tires were in shreds. On the last round the tatters were plainly visible. His pit crew had tried, vainly, to flag him down—to take a safe second place in a race he had never won—but they knew that Ralph would ignore the signal. DePalma was a giant—a racing giant whose vocabulary didn't contain the word quit.

Then from the backstretch, came the word—speeding faster than any mechanical device could repeat it—"DePalma has crashed. A tire blew out. He's badly hurt!" And then a car was coming. A cry went up. From out of the dust came the familiar pointed radiator. One tire was flat and pieces of rubber trailed the speeding machine, but straight and true it came to the finish line. It was DePalma. Forty-three seconds later the Mercer arrived. DePalma had his first Vanderbilt Cup!

Overdramatized? Hardly. Such happenings were commonplace as men raced over-horsepowered and under-constructed thunderbolts to fame, wealth and death shortly after the turn of the century. The Age of Giants, it has been called, and the young sporting giants who authored the deeds with their heroics helped to make a gigantic industry. The automobile had arrived!

Somehow, the story had been planted that only in Europe did real racing giants operate—that all great racing deeds were done either on the banks of the Rhine or the swift stretches of Brooklands—that Paris-Madrid was the Magna Charta of brave, dead race drivers, the home of the titled pilot, the beloved screwball. Not true. Not entirely true, that is, because here, in the land of the melting pot, suave and polished gentry died on speedways and strong men, as hard as the fourth-assistant spark plug holder in the Nazi Auto-Union racing team, rode over, under and through all opposition. Their stories have been neglected.

Take David Bruce-Brown. The name means little to moderns unless they're students of Indianapolis past-performance charts. If so, of course, the fellow with the hyphenated, odd last name will be recalled as finishing third in the first Hoosier 500. Bruce-Brown might be alive today if a left rear tire hadn't let go on a rough piece of country road near Milwaukee in 1912.

David, or "Davey" as his mother called him, was born of great wealth in New York. Like all young scions of the J. P. Morgan era, Davey had his choice of the ivy-growing colleges: Yale, Harvard or Princeton. He chose the first and to all appearances buried himself in thick books and an occasional fling at the Boola Boola song. Mater and Pater got the shock of their lives therefore on the morning of March 24, 1908. In blazing headlines they were told that their son had blistered the sands of Daytona Beach at 109 miles per hour. A family conference was scheduled.

Young David, with an exhibited distaste for ivy, had apprenticed himself as a mechanic to one "Cedrino," one-time chauffeur to the Queen of Spain, who was in this country, ostensibly, to race automobiles. Davey proved to be a better exercise jockey than a nut twister, so was given his chance to drive against the clock. A new world record was the result. Davey was a celebrity!

His next challenge was the 1911 American Grand Prix at Savannah. This international 411-mile road classic was assumed by many to be the private property of foreign drivers. At the end of the first lap on the moss-covered Georgia course the order was Wagner, Hemery, Nazzaro, Hanriot and Hautvast: France, Germany, France, Germany and France again. Against this array, the 23-year-old collegian, David Bruce-Brown gave battle. At the finish, after nearly six grueling hours, it was little Davey first and the favored Hemery second.

Bruce-Brown and DePalma went to Europe in 1912 and Davey led the French Grand Prix for three quarters of its distance until he ran out of gas and collected a disqualification. Then, while practicing for the Milwaukee Grand Prix, he was killed. A nasty story tying Teddy Tetzlaff to Davey's death survived the accident. Teddy, who carried the sobriquet of being the meanest race driver alive, happened to be near Davey on the road when the accident occurred. The tale made the rounds, and was believed, that Teddy had refused to give Davey racing room. The coroner didn't say so, however.

Tetzlaff, called "Terrible Teddy," was a character right out of the knights of the Middle Ages. A Westerner who rose from the masses to become the White Knight of California one day and the most despised black knight the next. Teddy was a madman behind the wheel and scoffed at danger. The great races he won—Santa Monica, Tacoma, Montamara—were not races, they were *chases!* Teddy neither slowed for curve nor traffic and the only way you could beat him was to lie back and await his misfortune.

Tetzlaff was unpredictable. At times he refused to race, then he might race only in the west and refuse to travel to the lucrative events eastward. The following season he was just as liable to show up at Elgin and Indianapolis and skip the Tacoma event. Despite his nature, however, manufacturers fought for his contract and endorsement. He took a car onto the Utah salt beds in 1914 (when no one was sure they would hold an automobile) and drove a measured mile at an average of 20 mph over the existing record. This,

36

in spite of his manager's instructions to merely *nudge* the record a bit. The manager, Bill Pickens, wanted to use the feat as a publicity gimmick, but Terrible Teddy would have none of the fakery. To him automobiles were made to be driven in only one manner—wide open.

Today it is hard to realize that in the Roaring Age of racing a major victory meant extra thousands of sales for the winning make of car. It was this fact which prompted one of the most hushed-up and spectacular kidnappings ever perpetrated. Tetzlaff was kidnapped and held for ransom just four days before an important race at Tacoma in 1912!

E. E. Hewlett, millionaire backer of the Fiat team and Teddy's contract holder at the time, paid the ransom and sent an emissary to escort his ace from his place of confinement to the race course. Teddy refused to leave, however! It seems he had formed a warm friendship with his captors —the inmates of one of the better establishments comprising Tacoma's red light district!

Tetzlaff won so many big races in 1912 and dominated the racing scene so completely that he might have easily been voted national champion. DePalma beat him in the Vanderbilt Cup however (after Tetzlaff had led up to 80 miles from the finish) and the AAA says DePalma was the 1912 champion by a margin of ten points. Teddy died a natural death in 1929—if a brain disturbance is called natural, that is.

California produced many racing giants during the Roaring Age. Frank Verbeck was one. A slight, beardless youth who looked so frail that track guards often refused to admit him to race courses, he nevertheless won so many races that his fame reached even the King of England. George V requested a telegraphic report of Verbeck's progress during every race and when he won the Los Angeles-Sacramento 444-mile city-to-city marathon, the British monarch wired his congratulations.

In 1911 Verbeck set the 24-hour record with 149 miles in a Fiat, topping the old British Brooklands record. Frank retired once, then attempted a comeback. His experience in that attempt put an end, forever, to his racing career.

Frank had deserted the sport at the request of his bride but the call of "just one more" Tacoma race was too great. As many young husbands do at least once in their lifetime, Verbeck invented a "business trip" that would take him away from home for a few days. The fabrication troubled him at first because his first-born child was scheduled soon to arrive, but activity at the track ended these thoughts and Frank was positive his secret was safe.

Late in the race Verbeck noted a great show of mirth and excitement in his pit as he raced by. The next time around he could see his blackboard hung out with a message. Slowing his pace to see the words, Frank read: IT'S A BOY!

Frank's retirement became permanent and he lives today in Pasadena where once a year he serves as a steward on the Mobilgas Economy Run. A co-steward on that run is Earl Cooper—and who can forget this great Stutz pilot who won everything but the Indianapolis 500 in a career that started in a despised Maxwell? Cooper—the California Comet—accumulated more AAA championship points than any other driver in history.

When Henry Stutz left the Marion Company to establish his own make of car, he brought with him a former riding mechanic named Gil Anderson. Anderson turned driver and put the Stutz in the limelight by finishing 11th in the first Indianapolis 500. Cooper then joined the Stutz team and wrote history. Anderson captured many of the classics in the east while Cooper was winning in the west. The public soon demanded a meeting between the two, and Stutz, over his better judgment, permitted a Cooper vs. Anderson race at the inaugural 500 mile classic at the Twin City Speedway, near Minneapolis, in 1915. This was a huge two-mile edifice that had cost a million dollars to construct. Everyone of note, including Oldfield, Burman, DePalma, O'Donnell and Mulford, wanted to win this first pot, but the newly laid cement took its toll on fragile tires and near the finish it was anyone's guess as to who held what position in the race—except in front. There rode the two Stutzes.

Cooper had made five tire stops and Anderson three. Their pit had scored them one lap apart, with Anderson leading, and the team more than eight miles in front of O'Donnell, in third. Cruising at half-throttle and side-by-side, the Stutz pilots asked for a position and lap count (a one-hand circular motion over the head). Stutz, wanting to verify his own scoring, made a hurried trip to the scoring stand where, to his amazement, he was told that his two aces were on the same lap and running only inches apart!

Now, the accepted rule for team managers says that drivers must be kept informed of position at all times. Still, knowing Cooper's and Anderson's competitive temperaments, Stutz was torn between duty, which would result in his two drivers racing each other—and the chance of both going over the wall—or flaunting tradition and saving first and second place in the very rich payoff.

Harry Stutz solved his problem in a novel manner. He stalled until his two cars came down the stretch, side-by-side, to start their last lap. Then, out came his signal board, reading: "POSITION?"

Cooper reacted first. Down went his throttle foot and—a fraction of an instant later—Anderson's. With identical power the two sailed through that last lap as if tied together. The initial Cooper momentum had carried him to a wheel-length advantage before Anderson's mount matched the rpm's. In this manner they crossed the finish line. The official times: Cooper 5.47:20.30; Anderson 5.47:20.55!

The year 1915 saw another close finish to a famous race. Match races were then in vogue as a method to settle arguments and some of the two-car dashes took on classic stature. Oldfield and DePalma would match skill at the drop of a pin—or a ten thousand dollar bill! The drivers always put up a side bet. When the gracious Italian eventually asserted his mastery over the great Barney, the latter's backers switched to Bob Burman. The Michigan youth had cemented a reputation as the speed king by taking Oldfield's discarded race cars and breaking Barney's own world records with them.

The meeting between these two giants was scheduled for the Sheepshead Bay two-mile board speedway in October, 1915. DePalma chose a 12-cylinder Sunbeam as his steed and Burman the famous old Blitzen Benz. The agreed distance was four miles—two laps of the giant bowl.

It proved to be a race of equal speed and when the pair flashed over the finish line, the judges looked like an Irish picnic at Duffey's pier. Some favored Burman, some DePalma, while a third faction held out for a dead heat. After much debate DePalma was announced the winner by the margin of one inch! But that was not the end. Into the turmoil at the top of the judges' stand strode DePalma. Shouting for attention, the silver-haired giant made himself heard. "As we crossed the finish line I was watching our front wheels. Bob was three inches in front!"

Burman is another gilded character out of racing's roaring age. He test-drove the first Buick ever built and, along with Louis Strang and the Chevrolet brothers, made up the Buick racing team when Buick dominated U. S. racing.

Of the original members of the famed Buick team, only

Louis Chevrolet died a natural death. Strang's death was most unspectacular for such a sensational performer. Like Bruce-Brown, Strang was a New Yorker of more than modest means. He was married to the Broadway queen of the period and was so astute and polished in his manners that the Case Motor Company hired him as a development engineer and race manager. Taking a Case touring model on a reliability run one day, Strang turned out for a horse and wagon on a back road near Blue River, Wisconsin. His speed was a mere four miles an hour, but when his right-front wheel hit the shoulder, the car toppled over. Strang was pinned underneath and soon died.

Racing history, from 1902 until the start of World War II, cannot be told without mentioning Barney Oldfield. "You-know-me-Barney" was the most famed throttle-twister of all time. Today he's an immortal, a legend. Hero deluxe and man without fear, he was racing's original bad boy with a persecution complex that few men have ever understood.

Many of Barney's escapades cannot be told in print. Each of his seven "life-time" suspensions from organized racing came with logical justification. Barney made and lost a dozen fortunes, but the former Toledo bellhop could never fully understand law and order. The first time AAA broke his back is a typical story. It involved Jack Johnson, another bad boy.

Johnson, as world heavyweight champion, was unpopular. His private life was hardly a text book for the advancement of colored peoples and, as a result, white hopes sprang from every corner of the earth. Johnson met the crusade by licking them all.

The heavyweight champion liked to drive fast cars and had a nasty habit of dusting crowds with his fast-moving runabout. This gave Oldfield a money-making idea. He challenged Johnson to a contest—not in the squared ring but on a race track—and billed himself as another white hope. Johnson, anxious for more worlds to conquer, accepted the challenge, declaring he would become the world's racing champion, as well. The AAA Contest Board branded the proposed match as a hoax and forbade Oldfield's participation on the grounds Johnson wasn't a licensed race driver. Whereupon a properly executed, signed and notarized race driver's license bearing the name of John Luther Johnson was produced. (A near-hysterical AAA office girl later admitted issuing such a license to a white man bearing that name.)

AAA promptly rescinded, suspended and declared the license null and void, but Barney, flaunting the dictum, raced anyway and before a tremendous and profitable crowd on Long Island made a sorry mess of Johnson's racing career. He won two five-mile heats in the ultra-slow time of 4:44 and 5:15. Johnson was more than a minute behind in the last heat. It was a fiasco of the first water, just as AAA said it would be.

Oldfield couldn't believe his personal popularity was overshadowed by law and order. He made a fortune running hippodromes in the cow country and never missed an opportunity to harass AAA. At the Vanderbilt Cup he showed up with a reporter's credentials. The police escorted him from the premises. At Toledo, once his home town, while Burman was in the process of breaking one of his world records, Barney sneaked into the infield, incognito, removed some fencing and drove onto the track in a Keystone comedy chase of the speeding Burman.

In later years, after he had been reduced to racing farm tractors in exhibitions, Barney, with a great show of emotion, accepted an appointment to the AAA Contest Board. The ink had hardly dried on his credentials, however, when he again let loose with a blast at the governing body. He served the shortest term ever recorded in the 40-year history of the Contest Board.

While "bad boys" are known in every sport, so too are the Ralph Mulfords. This mild-mannered Georgian was a master at the wheel of a Lozier, and later a Hudson. A Sunday school teacher, Mulford refused to race on the Sabbath, although most of the lucrative events were traditionally held on that day. In spite of this he copped the national driving crown twice and had over a hundred major victories to his credit.

Mulford was known as a man of refined habits and soft language. He always wore a starched white collar when racing. Despite his fine manners, it was a flash of Mulford's temper that resulted in an important racing rule that stands to this day, however. One of the favorites in the 1912 Indianapolis 500, Mulford, after being close to the lead all day, suffered such a serious mechanical breakdown that he was removed from contention. Re-entering the race during its late stages, the Georgian found himself a hopeless last. With nine cars across the finish line, Mulford was driving the only car remaining on the track. He then stopped at the finish line to ask if he had been awarded tenth position.

Carl Fisher, then president of the Indianapolis Speedway, gave him the answer: "Mr. Mulford, this race is for 500 miles. You will drive 500 miles or you won't get a cent!" Mulford drove off in a huff, stopped at his pit and ordered refreshments, then continued at a leisurely pace, much to the consternation of the tired, hungry and fatigued officials. The box score of the 1912 race tells the story. Mulford finished tenth—but two hours and 32 minutes after the winner. (That winter the rules were changed to give the chief steward power to terminate a race at his discretion.)

Eddie Hearne is officially remembered as the 1923 champion, but the little Chicago Irishman won road races before the first board speedway was ever constructed and set records on the Indianapolis Speedway when that famous plant was a dirt track.

Eddie remembers one experience he had "on the boards" which nearly put him on the water wagon for life. It happened at a time when board tracks were fast deteriorating as safe structures for speed. In fact, this particular track was so weather-beaten that large holes dotted the entire racing surface where rotting boards had fallen through or where contraction had separated plank ends. Little flags were placed at these danger spots and all a driver had to do during a race—besides stay upright at 150 mph— was drive an obstacle course around the flags!

Now prior to this particular race, urchins had discovered that by crawling under the old track they could stick their heads through the holes and thus afford themselves a worm's-eye, knot-hole view of the race. Naturally, they became adept at ducking when a car bore down on them!

Near the middle of the race, an accident occurred. Fred Wagner, the starter, slowed the cars until the wreckage was cleared, then sent the field away again, full speed. Hearne, near the front, had a good money position all but cinched when he suddenly cut his motor, crossed himself, and glided into the pit. Crawling slowly from the cockpit he waved his frantic mechanics away. "There's nothing wrong with the car," he declared, "I've just had enough. There's a dead man on the backstretch and we're kicking his head down that track!" Officials took off in a flurry of excitement to find the headless torso. It was never found, of course, for Eddie had seen only the bobbing heads of an urchin.

Perhaps the greatest driver of the roaring age is not remembered as a race driver at all simply because fate was fitting him for a greater role. Eddie Rickenbacker was about the toughest driver ever to saw an adversary off in a corner. Rick—as he is still called by his former racing associates—was definitely more than just another throttle flogger, as his racing record indicates.

Rickenbacker started his professional life as a secondary driver for a Columbus, Ohio, car manufacturer named Lee Frayer. Frayer was trying to promote and sell a questionable vehicle called the Firestone-Columbus by means of racing successes. He won a few races himself but once Rickenbacker got behind the wheel, the cars won with regularity. In fact, the future air ace wasn't too careful where and when he won and, consequently, found himself suspended for engaging in unsanctioned activity. Following a year "in the stands," Rickenbacker applied for reinstatement—and was turned down by the Contest Board.

When he finally did get back to racing, World War I had begun. Rickenbacker blazed to victory in two 300-mile races at Sioux City and in a 150-miler at Sheepshead Bay. Had these races been an Indianapolis 500 or a Vanderbilt Cup, Rickenbacker the race driver would have been remembered. Instead, the races died and were forgotten—and so were Rick's victories. He went directly from the cockpit of a Duesenberg to the cockpit of a Spad, and the rest is history. The world remembers Rickenbacker as the meteor who flashed over the skies of France, downing the despised Hun—but not as the race driver who was winning every automobile race in sight only 18 months before Black Jack Pershing called.

Yes, these men-boys were giants of the roaring age—giants whose names are all but forgotten but whose deeds wrote a brilliant chapter in the book of automobile racing.

WITH MOSS IN THE MILLE MIGLIA

by Denis Jenkinson

For all the great courage it takes to drive a racing car, there are more demanding pursuits. Of these, surely not the least is that of a co-*piloto*. Traveling just as fast as the man at the wheel, enduring just as many risks, he is, if anything, more to be applauded. For there is one important experience he *doesn't* share: the experience of being able to control the vehicle. When a man is actually driving a car, he has the comforting knowledge that he can, after all, pull to the side and stop, if he so desires. But the co-*piloto* can only ride, as a passenger, and at the mercy of not only the machine and road conditions, but of the race driver as well. Denis Jenkinson is perhaps the ideal fellow for the job. So far as anyone can tell, the bearded British journalist is entirely without fear. When "Jenks" elects to ride with a man, he trusts that man completely, in an almost, but not quite, mystical way (although he would look pained at the word). The extraordinary account of his ride with Stirling Moss, possibly the greatest driver who ever lived, follows below—without safety belt or roll bars.

On May 1, 1955, motor-racing history was made, for Stirling Moss won the 1,000-mile Mille Miglia, the first time in 22 years that this has been achieved by a British driver, and I had the very great privilege of sitting beside him throughout this epic drive.

But let us go back to the beginning, for this win was not a fluke on the spur of the moment, it was the result of weeks, even months, of preparation and planning. My enthusiasm for the Mille Miglia race goes back many years, among the reasons being the fact that it is permissible to carry a passenger, for this event is for all types of road-going cars, from family saloons to Grand Prix-type racing/sports cars, and when I had my first taste of the lure of the Mille Miglia as a competitor in 1954, with Abecassis in the HWM, I soon set about making plans for the 1955 event.

44

In '54, I enthused over a little private dice that Moss gave me in a Maserati, and at the time I mentioned to him my desire to run in the Mille Miglia again. Then in September, whilst in discussion with the American driver John Fitch, we came to the decision that the only way a non-Italian could win the Mille Miglia was by applying science. At the time he was hoping to be in the official Mercedes-Benz team for the event, and we had long talks about ways in which the driver could use a passenger as a mechanical brain, to remove the responsibility of learning the circuit. When it is realized that the race is over 1,000 miles of ordinary, unprepared Italian road, the only concession to racing being that all traffic is removed from the roads for the duration of the race, and the way through towns is lined with straw bales, it will be appreciated that the task of one man learning every corner, every swerve, gradient, hummock, brow and level-crossing is nigh impossible. Even the top Italian drivers, such as Taruffi, Maglioli, Castellotti, etc., only know sections of the route perfectly, and all the time they must concentrate on remembering what lies round the next corner, or over the next brow.

During the last winter, as is well known, Moss joined the Mercedes-Benz team and the firm decided that it would not be possible for Fitch to drive for them in the Mille Miglia, though he would be in the team for Le Mans, so all our plans looked like being of no avail. Then, just before Christmas, a telephone call from Moss invited me to be his passenger in the Mille Miglia in a Mercedes-Benz 300SLR, an invitation which I promptly accepted, John Fitch having sportingly agreed that it would be a good thing for me to try out our plans for beating the Italians with Moss as driver.

When I met Moss early in the new year to discuss the event I already had some definite plan of action. Over lunch it transpired that he had very similar plans, of using the passenger as a second brain to look after navigation, and when we pooled our accumulated knowledge and ideas a great deal of ground work was covered quickly. From four previous Mille Miglia races with Jaguars Moss had gathered together a good quantity of notes, about bumpy level-crossings, blind hill-brows, dangerous corners and so on, and as I knew certain sections of the course intimately, all this knowledge put down on paper amounted to about 25 per cent of the circuit.

Early in February Mercedes-Benz were ready to start practicing, the first outing being in the nature of a test for the prototype 300SLR, and we completed two laps, including having an accident. While doing this testing I made copious notes, some of them rather like Chinese due to trying to write at 150 mph, but when we stopped for lunch, or for the night, we spent the whole time discussing the roads we had covered and transcribing my notes. The things we concentrated on were places where we might break the car, such as very bumpy railway-crossings, sudden dips in the road, bad surfaces, tramlines and so on. Then we logged all the difficult corners, grading them as "saucy ones," "dodgy ones" and "very dangerous ones," having a hand sign to indicate each type. Then we logged slippery surfaces, using another hand sign, and as we went along Moss indicated his interpretation of the conditions, while I pinpointed the place by a kilometer stone, plus or minus. Our task was eased greatly by the fact that there is a stone at every kilometer on Italian roads, and they are numbered in huge black figures, facing on-coming traffic.

In addition to all the points round the course where a mistake might mean an accident, and there are hundreds of them, we also logged all the long straights and everywhere that we could travel at maximum speed even though visibility was restricted, and again there were dozens of such points. Throughout all this preliminary work Moss impressed upon me at every possible moment the importance of not making any mistakes, such as indicating a brow to be flat-out when in reality it was followed by a tight left-hand bend. I told him he need not worry, as any accident he might have was going to involve me as well, as I was going to be by his side until the race was finished. After our first practice session we sorted out all our notes and had them typed out into some semblance of order, and before leaving England again I spent hours with a friend, checking and cross-checking, going over the whole list many times, finally being 100 per cent certain that there were no mistakes.

On our second visit to Italy for more laps of the circuit, we got down to fine details, grading some corners as less severe and others as much more so, especially as now we knew the way on paper it meant that we arrived at many points much faster than previously when reconnoitring the route. On another lap I went the whole way picking out really detailed landmarks that I would be able to see no matter what the conditions, whether we had the sun in our eyes or it was pouring with rain, and for this work we found Moss' Mercedes-Benz 220A saloon most useful as it would cruise at an easy 85 mph and at the same time we could discuss any details.

Our whole plan was now nearing completion, we had 17 pages of notes, and Moss had sufficient confidence in me to take blind brows at 90-100, believing me when I said the road went straight on; though he freely admitted that he was not sure whether he would do the same thing at 170 mph in the race, no matter how confident I was. He said he'd probably ease back to 160 for, though that 10 mph would make no difference to the resulting crash if I had made a mistake, it comforted him psychologically! Throughout all this training we carefully kept a log of our running time and average speeds, and some of them were positively indecent, and certainly not for publication, but the object was to find out which parts of the 1,000 miles dropped the overall average and where we could make up time, and our various averages in the 220A, the 300 SL and the 300SLR gave us an extremely interesting working knowledge of how the Mille Miglia might be won or lost.

Our second practice period ended in another accident and this time a smashed 300SL coupe, for Italian army lorries turn across your bows without warning just as English ones do. Rather crestfallen, we anticipated the rage of team-chief Neubauer when we reported this second crash, but his only worry was that we were not personally damaged; the crashed car was of no importance; these things happened to everyone and anyway their only interest was to win the Mille Miglia, regardless of cost.

Leaving Italy for another brief respite, we both worried-out every detail we could think about, from every aspect, the car, the route, our hand signals—for we could not converse in the 300SLR—any emergencies that might arise, anywhere we could save seconds, details of our own personal comfort which would avoid fatigue, and so on. We lived and breathed Mille Miglia day in and day out, leaving no idea untried. The joy of all this was that Daimler-Benz were doing exactly the same things on the mechanical side, supervised by engineers Uhlenhaut, Kosteletsky and Werner, while the racing department were working unceasingly and Neubauer was worrying-out every detail of the race-organization in Italy. We were putting all our efforts into this race, knowing that they were negligible in comparison with those of the factory.

After Easter we went out to Brescia for our third and final practicing session, the technical department, with Kling and Herrmann, having already made an extra one. During their practice period they had thrashed the prototype car up and down the section from Rome to Florence, for this part of the route was the hardest. There are few straights, but all the time the car is averaging nearly 100 mph, the chassis being subjected to strains from every possible angle, and as the 58-gallon petrol tank would be full when leaving Rome, this part of the route would be the most likely on which a breakdown would occur.

By now our details of the route were perfected and I now wrote them all down on a special sheet of paper eighteen feet in length. Moss had had an alloy case made, on the map-roller system, and for our final practice I employed this machine, winding the paper from the lower roller to the upper one, the notes being read through a Perspex window, sealed with Sellotape in the event of the race being run in rain. A complete lap in a 300SL was done as a sort of dress rehearsal, this car being ideal as it had a maximum of nearly 140, good acceleration, and was a very good approach to racing conditions, while at the same time we could speak to each other if the need arose, though normally all our conversation was done by hand signals, there being about 15 altogether, to cover every aspect of conversation. During this dress rehearsal we employed an amusing technique in the more deserted parts of the route, especially in the mountains, where I kept an eye on the approaching road out of the side windows, and even out of the rear one on mountain hairpins and, by continually shouting "Yes" while the road was clear, Moss could have a real go at "nine-tenths" on the section of road just in front of him, certain in the knowledge that no traffic was approaching, for it must be remembered that all our practice was being done on normal Italian roads, open to the public. This technique, while being amusing to us, was also useful to Moss as it meant he could get the feel of the road surface conditions at racing speeds. By now the Mille Miglia date was approaching and all round the 1,000 miles we saw more and more signs of growing enthusiasm, occasionally seeing other competitors practicing parts of the route, while the police were beginning to leap off the pavement, stop the traffic and wave us on over crossroads with excited cries of "Mille Miglia—via!" and, of course, the Italian populace were leaping straight up into the air with joy as Moss fought the sliding SL through many of the corners. It was interesting that the average English enthusiast would turn his head and look if he saw a 300SL being really motored, whereas the Italians, from errand boys to bank managers, will spontaneously leave the ground and spin completely round, with excited waves, at the same sight, and then rush to another point in the hope of getting a further glimpse of the speeding car. We completed our third practice period without any crashes, though the "hack" SLR decided to give-up-the-ghost while we were having a final run in it, but we were entirely blameless; old age creeps on the best vehicles, and this one had done the equivalent of at least six Mille Miglias in the hands of Moss, Fangio, Kling and Herrmann, the four drivers for the race.

A week before the event we went to Stuttgart to try out the actual car we were using in the race, and several laps of the fast Hockenheim circuit convinced us that we had a truly magnificent 3-litre sports car under us, the eight-cylinder fuel-injection engine giving well over 290 bhp on normal pump petrol, and the car geared to give a maximum of 170 mph at the peak revolutions of 7,500 rpm, though we were given no ultimate limit, should the car wind itself over this downhill. On this SLR the seats were made to measure for us, being cut-and-shut just like a tailor would make a suit, while every detail in the cockpit received our personal attention, and anything was altered to our desire without question. When we finally left the racing department at 5 P.M. on Tuesday, April 26th, we had the pleasant feeling that we had just left an organization that knew no limit to the trouble they would go to in order that we might start the Mille Miglia with everything on our side.

Next day we flew to Brescia and when we went round to the garage in the evening the cars were already there, having been driven down in the fast racing lorries overnight. We were now satisfied with almost everything we could think about; we had practiced wheel-changing over and over again, in case we had tire trouble, and I would add that we impressed the Mercedes-Benz mechanics by changing a rear wheel in 1 min. 25 sec. from stopping the car to starting off again. We had practiced fitting the temporary aluminum air-screens that went in front of the Perspex screen should it be broken by a stone—Mercedes-Benz engineers remembering how Hermann Lang was nearly suffocated at 170 at Donington Park in 1938 when his windscreen was broken. We had tried changing plugs; we had studied the details of the pipes of the fuel-injection, the petrol pumps, various important parts of the wiring system, how the bonnet catches

49

functioned; we were given spare ignition keys, shown where numerous small spares were stowed should we stop by the roadside with minor trouble; and by the end of the week we felt extremely confident that we could give of our best in this toughest of motor races, lasting for more than 10 hours over every known road condition, over mountains and through cities, for 1,000 miles.

On the Friday before the race we did a final test on the nearby Autostrada, to try out some windscreen modifications to improve the air-flow along the cockpit sides. Also Moss tried out a new mechanism fitted to the gear-change that would prevent him from changing from second gear to fifth gear. The gear-gate is exposed, with first left-forward, second center-rear, third center forward, fourth right-rear, and fifth right-forward. Being used to four-speed boxes Moss was occasionally going across the gate from second to fifth, and when he told the engineers about this the racing department set to and designed, drew and made an entirely fool-proof link-mechanism that fitted on the top of the gate that would prevent this. He mentioned this on Tuesday afternoon and on Friday morning the new parts arrived in Brescia and he was trying the mechanism out before lunch—at such speed does a true racing department work.

For the week before the race I had been going to bed extremely early and getting up extremely early, a complete reversal of my normal life, for to suddenly get up at 6 A.M. gives me a feeling of desolation until well past mid-morning. Moss had been employing similar tactics, so that when we went down to the start at 6:30 A.M. on the morning of May 1st we were both feeling ready for anything.

All the previous week a truly Italian sun had blazed out of the sky every day and reports assured us that race-day would be perfectly dry and hot, so we anticipated race speeds being very high. I had a list of the numbers of all our more serious rivals, as well as many of our friends in slower cars, and also the existing record times to every control point round the course, so that we would have an idea of how we were doing. We had privately calculated on an average of 90 mph—2 mph over the record of Marzotto, providing the car went well and the roads were dry. Mercedes-Benz gave us no orders, leaving the running of the race entirely to each driver, but insisting that the car was brought back to Brescia if humanly possible. Moss and I had made a pact that we would keep the car going as long as was practicable having decided in practice at which point

50

we could have the engine blow-up and still coast in to the finish, and how many kilometers we were prepared to push it to finish or to a control. At Ravenna, Pescara, Rome, Florence and Bologna there were Mercedes-Benz pits, complete with all spares, changes of tires should it start to rain, food, drink and assistance of every sort, for in this race there are no complicated rules about work done on the car or outside assistance; it is a free-for-all event.

The enormous entry had started to leave Brescia the previous evening at 9 P.M., while we were sleeping peacefully, the cars leaving at 1-min. intervals, and it was not until 6:55 A.M. on Sunday morning that the first of the over-2,000-c.c. sports cars left. It was this group that held the greatest interest, for among the 34 entries lay the outright winner of this race, though many of the 2-liter Maseratis and smaller Oscas and Porsches could not be overlooked. Starting positions were arranged by ballot beforehand and the more important to us were: Fangio 658, Kling 701, Collins (Aston Martin) 702, Herrmann 704, Maglioli (Ferrari) 705; then there went off a group of slower cars, and Carini (Ferrari) 714, Scotti (Ferrari) 718, Pinzero (Ferrari) 720, and then us at 7:22 A.M. There was no hope of seeing our team-mates, for they left too long before us, as did Maglioli, but we were hoping to catch Carini before the end. Our big worry was not so much those in front, but those behind, for there followed Castellotti (Ferrari 4.4-liter) 723, Sighinolfi (Ferrari 3.7-liter) 724, Paulo Marzotto (Ferrari 3.7-liter) 727 and, finally, the most dangerous rival of them all, that master tactician, Taruffi (Ferrari 3.7-liter) 728. With all these works Ferraris behind us we could not hang about in the opening stages, for Castellotti was liable to catch us, and Sighinolfi would probably scrabble past us using the grass banks, he being that sort of driver, and Marzotto would stop at nothing to beat the German cars, so if we didn't press on straight away there was a good chance of the dice becoming a little exciting, not to say dangerous, in the opening 200 miles.

Neubauer was ever present at the start, warning Moss to give the car plenty of throttle as he left the starting ramp, for Herrmann had nearly fluffed his take-off; he also assured us that we could take the dip at the bottom of the ramp without worrying about grounding. The mechanics had warmed the engine and they pushed it up onto the starting platform to avoid unnecessary strain on the single-plate clutch, one of the weak points of the 300SLR. The route-card which we had to get stamped at the various controls round the course was securely attached to a board and already fitted in its special holder, the board being attached by a cord to one of my grab-rails, to avoid losing it in the excitement of any emergency. We both settled down in our seats, Moss put his goggles on, I showed him a note at the top of my roller device, warning him not to apply the brakes fiercely on the first corner, for the bi-metal drums needed a gentle application to warm them after standing for two days.

Thirty seconds before 7:22 A.M. he started the engine, the side exhaust pipes blowing a cloud of smoke over the starter and Sig. Castegnato and Count Maggi, the two men behind this great event, and then as the flag fell we were off with a surge of acceleration and up to peak revs. in first, second and third gears, weaving our way through the vast crowds lining the sides of the road. Had we not been along this same road three times already in an SLR amid the hurly-burly of morning traffic, I should have been thoroughly frightened, but now, with the roads clear ahead of us, I thought Moss could really get down to some uninterrupted motoring. We had the sun shining full in our eyes, which made navigating difficult, but I had written the notes over and over again, and gone over the route in my imagination so many times that I almost knew it by heart, and one of the first signals was to take a gentle S-bend through a village on full throttle in fourth gear, and as Moss did this, being quite unable to see the road for more than 100 yards ahead, I settled down to the job, confident that our scientific method of equalling -the Italians' ability at open-road racing was going to work. At no time before the race did we ever contemplate getting into the lead, for we fully expected Fangio to set the pace, with Kling determined to win at all costs, so we were out for a third place, and to beat all the Ferraris. Barely 10 miles after the start we saw a red speck in front of us and had soon nipped by on a left-hand curve. It was 720, Pinzero, number 721 being a non-starter. By my right hand was a small grab-rail and a horn button, the steering was on the left of the cockpit, by the way, and this button not only blew the horn, but also flashed the lights, so that while I played a fanfare on this Moss placed the car for overtaking other competitors. My direction indications I was giving with my left hand, so what with turning the map roller and feeding Moss with sucking sweets there was never a dull moment. The car was really going well now, and on the straights to Verona we were getting 7,500 in top gear, a speed

of 274 kph or as close to 170 mph as one could wish to
travel. On some of these long straights our navigation system
was paying handsomely, for we could keep at 170 over
blind brows, even when overtaking slower cars, Moss sure in
the knowledge that all he had to do was to concentrate
on keeping the car on the road and travelling as fast as
possible. This in itself was more than enough, but he was
sitting back in his usual relaxed position, making no apparent effort, until some corners were reached when the
speed at which he controlled slides, winding the wheel from
right to left and back again, showed that his superb reflexes and judgment were on top of their form.

Cruising at maximum speed, we seemed to spend most of
the time between Verona and Vicenza passing Austin-
Healeys that could not have been doing much more than
115 mph, and, with flashing light, horn blowing and a
wave of the hand, we went by as though they were touring.
Approaching Padova Moss pointed behind and I looked round
to see a Ferrari gaining on us rapidly, and with a grimace
of disgust at one another we realized it was Castellotti. The
Mercedes-Benz was giving all it had, and Moss was driving
hard but taking no risks, letting the car slide just so far on
the corners and no more. Entering the main street of Padova
at 150, we braked for the right-angled bend at the end,
and suddenly I realized that Moss was beginning to work
furiously on the steering wheel, for we were arriving at the
corner much too fast and it seemed doubtful whether we
could stop in time. I sat fascinated, watching Moss working
away to keep control, and I was so intrigued to follow his
every action and live every inch of the way with him, that I
completely forgot to be scared. With the wheels almost on
locking-point he kept the car straight to the last possible
fraction of a second, making no attempt to get round the
corner, for that would have meant a complete spin and
then anything could happen. Just when it seemed we must
go head-on into the straw bales Moss got the speed low
enough to risk letting go the brakes and try taking the
corner, and as the front of the car slid over the dry road we
went *bump!* into the bales with our left-hand front corner,
bounced off into the middle of the road and, as the car was
then pointing in the right direction, Moss selected bottom
gear and opened out again.

All this time Castellotti was right behind us, and as we
bounced off the bales he nipped by us, grinning over his
shoulder. As we set off after him, I gave Moss a little hand-

clap of appreciation for showing me just how a really great driver acts in a difficult situation.

Through Padova we followed the 4.4-liter Ferrari and on acceleration we could not hold it, but the Italian was driving like a maniac, sliding all the corners, using the pavements and the loose edges of the road. Round a particularly dodgy left-hand bend on the outskirts of the town I warned Moss and then watched Castellotti sorting out his Ferrari, the front wheels on full understeer, with the inside one off the ground, and rubber pouring off the rear tires, leaving great wide marks on the road. This was indeed motor-racing from the best possible position, and beside me was a quiet, calm young man who was following the Ferrari at a discreet distance, ready for any emergency. Out of the town we joined an incredibly fast stretch of road, straight for many miles, and we started alongside the Ferrari in bottom gear, but try as the Mercedes-Benz did the red car just drew away from us, and once more Moss and I exchanged very puzzled looks. By the time we had reached our maximum speed the Ferrari was over 200 yards ahead, but then it remained there, the gap being unaltered along the whole length of the straight. At the cut-off point at the end we gained considerably, both from the fact that we knew exactly when the following left-hand corner was approaching and also from slightly superior brakes. More full-throttle running saw us keeping the Ferrari in sight, and then as we approached a small town we saw Castellotti nip past another Ferrari, and we realized we were going to have to follow through the streets, until there was room to pass. It was number 714, Carini, so soon, and this encouraged Moss to run right round the outside of the Ferrari, on a right-hand curve, confident from my signals that the road would not suddenly turn left. This very brief delay had let Castellotti get away from us but he was not completely out of sight, and after waving to Peter Collins, who had broken down by the roadside before Rovigo, we went into that town at terrific speed. Straight across the square we went, where in practice we had had to go round the island; broadside we left the last right turn of the town, with the front wheels on full opposite lock and the throttle pedal hard down. Castellotti was in sight once more but out on the open roads he was driving so near the limit that on every corner he was using the gravel and rough stuff on the edges of the road. This sent up a huge cloud of dust, and we could never be sure whether or not we were going to enter it to find the Ferrari sideways across the road, or bouncing off the banks and trees, for this sort of hazard a scientific route-navigating method could not cope with. Wisely, Moss eased back a little and the Ferrari got ahead of us sufficiently to let the dust clouds settle.

Along the new road by the side of the River Po we overtook Lance Macklin in his Austin-Healey, and he gave us a cheery wave, and then we went through Ferrara, under the railway bridge, over the traffic lights and down the main streets and out onto the road to Ravenna. All the way along there were signs of people having the most almighty incidents, black marks from locked wheels making the weirdest patterns on the road, and many times on corners we had signalled as dangerous or dodgy we came across cars in the touring categories lying battered and bent by the roadside, sure indication that our grading of the corner was not far wrong. To Ravenna the road winds a great deal and now I could admire the Moss artistry as he put in some very steady "nine-tenth" motoring, especially on open bends round which he could see and on those that he knew, and the way he would control the car with throttle and steering wheel long after all four tires had reached the breakaway point was a sheer joy, and most difficult to do justice to with a mere pen and paper. Approaching the Ravenna control I took the route-card board from its holder, held it up for Moss to see, to indicate that we had to stop here to receive the official stamp, and then as we braked towards the "CONTROLLO" banner across the road, and the black and white chequered line on the road itself, amid waving flags and numerous officials, I held my right arm well out of the car to indicate to them which side we wanted the official with the rubber stamp to be. Holding the board on the side of the cockpit we crossed the control line, *bang!* went the rubber stamp, and we were off without actually coming to rest. Just beyond the control were a row of pits and there was 723, Castellotti's Ferrari, having some tire changes, which was not surprising in view of the way he had been driving.

With a scream of "Castellotti!" Moss accelerated hard round the next corner and we twisted our way through the streets of Ravenna, nearly collecting an archway in the process, and then out on the fast winding road to Forli. Our time to Ravenna had been well above the old record but Castellotti had got there before us and we had no idea how Taruffi and the others behind us were doing. Now Moss continued the pace with renewed vigor and we went through

Forli, waving to the garage that salvaged the SL we crashed in practice, down the fast winding road to Rimini, with another wave to the Alfa Romeo service station that looked after the SLR that broke its engine. I couldn't help thinking that we had certainly left our mark round the course during practice. Ever since leaving the start we had had the rising sun shining in our eyes and, now, with the continual effects of sideways "G" on my body, my poor stomach was beginning to suffer and, together with the heat from the gearbox by my left buttock, the engine fumes, and the nauseating brake-lining smells from the inboard-mounted brakes, it cried "enough" and what little breakfast I had eaten went overboard, together with my spectacles, for I made the fatal mistake of turning my head sideways at 150 mph with my goggles lowered. Fortunately, I had a spare pair, and there was no time to worry about a protesting stomach, for we were approaching Pesaro, where there was a sharp right corner.

Now the calm, blue Adriatic sea appeared on our left and we were on the long coastal straights, taking blind brows, and equally blind bridges at our full 170, and I chuckled to myself as I realized that Moss was not lifting his foot as he had threatened. We were beginning to pass earlier numbers very frequently now, among them some 2-liter Maseratis being driven terribly slowly, a couple of TR2 Triumphs running in convoy, and various saloons, with still numerous signs of the telling pace, a wrecked Giulietta on the right, a 1,100-c.c. Fiat on the left, a Ferrari coupe almost battered beyond recognition and a Renault that had been rolled up into a ball. Through Ancona the crowds were beautifully controlled, barriers keeping them back on the pavements, and we were able to use the full width of the road everywhere, and up the steep hill leaving the town we stormed past more touring-car competitors who had left in the small hours of the morning while we were still asleep. All this time there had been no signs of any of our close rivals. We had passed the last of the Austin-Healeys, driven by Abecassis, a long way back, and no Ferraris had appeared in our rear-view mirror.

It was a long way down to the next control point, at Pescara, and we settled down to cruising at our maximum speed, the car giving no impression at all of how fast it was travelling, until we overtook another competitor, who I knew must be doing 110, when I looked sideways at the trees and hedges flashing past. It was now mid-morning and the sun was well above us but still shining down onto our faces and making the cockpit exceedingly hot, in spite of having all the air vents fully open. Through the dusty, dirty Adriatic villages we went and all the time I gave Moss the invaluable hand signals that were taking from him the mental strain of trying to remember the route, though he still will not admit to how much mental strain he suffered convincing himself that I was not making any mistakes in my 170 mph navigation. On one straight, lined with trees, we had marked down a hump in the road as being "flat-out" only if the road was dry. It was, so I gave the appropriate signal and with 7,500 rpm in fifth gear on the tachometer we took off, for we had made an error in our estimation of the severity of the hump. For a measurable amount of time the vibro-massage that you get sitting in a 300SLR at that speed suddenly ceased, and there was time for us to look at each other with raised eyebrows before we landed again. Even had we been in the air for only one second we should have travelled some 200 feet through the air, and I estimated the "duration of flight" at something more than one second. The road was dead straight and the Mercedes-Benz made a perfect four-point landing and I thankfully praised the driver that he didn't move the steering wheel a fraction of an inch, for that would have been our end. With the heat of the sun and the long straights we had been getting into a complacent stupor, but this little "moment" brought us back to reality and we were fully on the job when we approached Pescara. Over the level crossing we went, far faster than we had ever done in practice, and the car skated right across the road, with all four wheels sliding, and I was sure we were going to write-off some petrol pumps by the roadside, but somehow "the boy" got control again and we merely brushed some straw bales and then braked heavily to a stop for the second control stamp. Approaching this point I not only held the route-card for the driver to see, but also pointed to the fuel filler, for here we were due to make our first refuelling. However, I was too late, Moss was already pointing backwards at the tank himself to tell me the same thing. Just beyond the control line we saw engineer Werner holding a blue flag bearing the Mercedes-Benz star and as we stopped everything happened at once. Some 18 gallons of fuel went in from a gravity tank, just suf-ficient to get us to our main stop at Rome, the windscreen was cleaned for it was thick with dead flies, a hand gave me a slice of orange and a peeled banana, while another was holding a small sheet of paper, someone else was looking at the tires and Moss still had the engine running. On the paper was written "Taruffi, Moss 15 seconds, Herrmann, Kling, Fangio," and their times; I had just yelled "second, 15 seconds behind Taruffi" when I saw a uniformed arm trying to switch off the ignition. I recognized an interfering police arm and gave it a thump, and as I did so, Moss crunched in bottom gear and we accelerated away as hard as we could go. What had seemed like an age was actually only 28 seconds!

Over the bridge we went, sharp right and then up one of the side turnings of Pescara towards the station, where we were to turn right again. There was a blue Gordini just going round the corner and then I saw that we were overshooting and with locked wheels we slid straight on, *bang* into the straw bales. I just had time to hope there was nothing solid behind the wall of bales when the air was full of flying straw and we were on the pavement. Moss quickly selected bottom gear and without stopping he drove along the pavement behind the bales, until he could bounce down off the curb and continue on his way, passing the Gordini in the process. As we went up through the gears on the long straight out of Pescara, I kept an eye on the water temperature gauge, for that clonk certainly creased the front of the car, and may have damaged the radiator, or filled the intake with straw, but all seemed well, the temperature was still remaining constant. There followed three completely blind brows in quick succession and we took these at full speed, the effect being rather like a switchback at a fair, and then we wound and twisted our way along the barren valley between the rocky mountain sides, to Popoli, where a Bailey Bridge still serves to cross a river. Along this valley I saw the strange sight of about 50 robed monks, with shining bald pates, standing on a high mound and waving to us as we went by with a noise sufficient to wake the devil himself. Up into the mountains we climbed, sliding round the hairpins with that beautiful Moss technique, and then along the peculiar deserted plateau high up in the mountains we held our maximum speed for many kilometers, to be followed by a winding twisting road into Aquila, where up the main street the control was dealt with while still on the move. We certainly were not wasting any seconds anywhere and Moss was driving absolutely magnificently, right on the limit of adhesion all the time, and more often than not over the limit, driving in that awe-inspiring narrow margin that you enter just before you have a crash if you have not the Moss skill, or those few yards of momentary terror you have on ice just before you go in the ditch. This masterly handling was no fluke, he was doing it deliberately, his extra special senses and reflexes allowing him to go that much closer to the absolute limit than the average racing driver and way beyond the possibilities of normal mortals like you or me.

On the way to Rome we hit a level crossing that had been just "bumpy" in the SL and smooth in the 220A; the resultant thud threw us high out of our seats into the airstream, and with a crash we landed back again, nearly breaking our spines, but the Mercedes-Benz suspension absorbed it all without protest and there was no feeling that anything had "bottomed" unduly severely. This sort of thing had happened three or four times already, for our route-noting was not infallible, and it seemed unbelievable that nothing broke on the car each time. Although we occasionally saw a train streaming along in the distance we never came across any closed level crossings, though if we had, we had a remedy. In practice we had tried lifting the barrier, Italian gates being two long poles that lower across the road, and found that the slack on the operating cables was just sufficient to allow the car to be driven under the pole, much to the annoyance of the crossing-keeper. However, this did not arise and down into the Rome control we had a pretty clear run, being highly delighted to overtake Maglioli soon after Rieti, he suffering from an arm injury received in practice, and a car that was not going well. With a grin at each other we realized that one of our unseen rivals was now disposed of, but we still had Taruffi behind us on the road, and no doubt well ahead of us on time, for all this ground was local color to him. Coming down off the mountains we had overtaken Musso driving a 2-liter Maserati and as we had calculated that we were unlikely ever to catch him, if we averaged 90 mph for the whole race, we realized we must be setting a fantastic record speed, but as Taruffi had been leading at Pescara, his average must be even higher.

The last six miles into the Rome control were an absolute nightmare; there were no corners that needed signals, and we would normally have done 150-160, but the crowds of spectators were so thick that we just could not see the road and the surface being bumpy Moss dared not drive much over 130 for there was barely room for two cars abreast. It seemed that the whole of Rome was out to watch the race, and all oblivious of the danger of a high-speed rac-

59

ing car. While I blew the horn and flashed the lights Moss swerved the car from side to side and this had the effect of making those on the very edge leap hastily backwards, thus giving us a little more room. The last mile into the control was better oganized and I was able to show Moss the control card, point backwards at the fuel tank and also at the fibre disc wired to the steering column which had to be punched at this control. *Bang* went the stamp and we then drew into the Mercedes-Benz pit and switched off the engine; this was our first real stop since leaving Brescia nearly 3½ hours ago, and our average speed to this point was 107 mph, the average to Pescara having been 118, the mountain section causing it to drop from there to Rome.

As we stopped Moss leapt out to relieve himself. I felt the car rise up on the jacks and heard the rear hub nuts being beaten off, the windscreen was cleaned and a welcome shower of water sprinkled over me, for I was very hot, very tired, very dirty, oily and sweaty and must have looked a horrible sight to spectators. The fuel tank was being filled, someone handed me a drink of mineral water and an orange, and offered a tray of sandwiches and cakes, but I felt incapable of eating anything firmer than a slice of orange. A hand appeared in front of me holding a sheet of paper and I snatched it and read "Moss, Taruffi, Herrmann, Kling, Fangio" and the times showed we had a lead of nearly two minutes. *Bump* went the car as it was dropped down off the jacks, and with a lithe bound Moss was into the driving seat again and as we took the hairpin after the control I managed to yell in his ear "First by more than one minute from Taruffi" and then the noise of the exhaust and wind prevented any further words. On the next bend we saw a silver Mercedes-Benz, number 701, well off the road among the trees and badly wrecked. We knew it was Kling and exchanged long faces with each other, wondering how badly hurt he was, but this had no effect on Moss and he now began to put everything he knew into his driving, on this most difficult section, while I had to concentrate hard in order to give him warnings and signals of the approaching road conditions, for this was indeed a difficult section for both of us. Past Monterosi we waved to the "Agip" service station, where we had a sheep-killing incident in practice, and then we sped on our way through Bitterbo, sliding this way and that, leaving the ground on more occasions than I can remember, yet all the while feeling completely at ease, for such is the confidence that Moss gave me, and round the corners I never ceased to marvel at the superb judgment with which he weighed up the maximum possible speed at which he could go, and just how far he could let the car slide without going into the ditch or hitting a wall or rock face. Now there was the continual hazard of passing slower cars, though it must be recorded that most of them gave way splendidly, keeping one eye on the mirror. Just after Acquapendente I made my first and only mistake in navigating, that it was not serious is why you are reading these words now; having just given warning of a very dodgy right-hand bend I received a shower of petrol down my neck and looking round to see what had happened we arrived at another similar corner, and I missed the signal. Fortunately Moss had recognized the corner, for he knew many parts of the course extremely well, and after seeing that the petrol was coming from the filler due to surge, I looked back to see an irate Moss face saying very rude things at me and shaking his fist, all the while cornering at a fantastic speed. How serious the fuel surge was I did not know, and as the exhaust pipes were on the side of the car I decided it would be all right and said nothing to Moss, as he appeared not to have received any of the spray. For the next 10 or 15 miles I received this gentle spray of cold fuel, cooling in the enormous heat of the cockpit, but a little worrying in case it got worse. Up the Radicofani Pass we stormed and the way the car leapt and slithered about would have really frightened me had I not already had a lot of experience of its capabilities and of the skill of Stirling Moss; as it was I sat there and revelled in the glorious feeling of really fast motoring. Over the top of the pass we swept past a saloon car competitor, into a downhill right-hand bend followed by a sharp left-hander. Now, previous to this Moss had been pointing to the front of the car and indicating that a brake was beginning to grab on occasions, and this was one of them. Without any warning the car spun and there was just time to think what a desolated part of Italy in which to crash, when I realized that we had almost stopped in our own length and were sliding gently into the ditch to land with a crunch that dented the tail. "This is all right," I thought, "we can probably push it out of this one," and I was about to start getting out when Moss selected bottom gear and we drove out—lucky indeed! Before we could point the car in the right direction we had to make two reverses and as we accelerated away down the mountain side, I fiddled about putting the safety catch back on the reverse position of the gear-gate, while we poked our tongues out at each other in mutual derision.

At the Siena control we had no idea of whether we were still leading or not, but Moss was quite certain that Taruffi would have had to have worked extremely hard to catch him, for he had put all he knew into that last part of the course, he told me afterwards. Never relaxing for an instant he continued to drive the most superb race of his career, twirling the steering wheel this way and that, controlling slides with a delicateness of throttle that was fairy-like, or alternately provoking slides with the full power of the engine, in order to make the car change direction bodily, the now dirty, oily and battered collection of machinery that had left Brescia gleaming like new still answering superbly to his every demand, the engine always being taken to 7,500 rpm in the gears, and on one occasion to 8,200, the excitement at that particular instant not allowing time for a gear change or an easing of the throttle, for the way Moss steered the car round the sharp corners with the back wheels was sheer joy to experience.

On the winding road from Siena to Florence physical strain began to tell on me, for with no steering wheel to give me a feel of what the car was going to do, my body was being continually subjected to terrific centrifugal forces as the car changed direction. The heat, fumes and noise were becoming almost unbearable, but I gave myself renewed energy by looking at Stirling Moss who was sitting beside me, completely relaxed, working away at the steering as if we had only just left Brescia, instead of having been driving for nearly 700 miles under a blazing sun. Had I not known the route I would have happily got out there and then, having enjoyed every mile, but ahead lay some interesting roads over which we had practiced hard, and the anticipation of watching Moss really try over these stretches, with the roads closed to other traffic, made me forget all about the physical discomforts. I was reminded a little of the conditions when we approached one corner and some women got up and fled with looks of terror on their faces, for the battered Mercedes-Benz, dirty and oil-stained and making as much noise as a Grand Prix car, with two sweaty, dirty, oil-stained figures behind the windscreen, must have looked terrifying to peaceful peasants, as it entered the corner in a full four-wheel slide. The approaches of Florence were almost back-breaking as we bounced and leapt over the badly maintained roads, and across the tramlines, and my heart went out to the driver of an orange Porsche who was hugging the crown of the steeply cambered road. He must have been shaken as we shot past with the left-hand wheels right down in the gutter. Down a steep hill in second gear we went, into third at peak revs., and I thought "It's a brave man who can unleash nearly 300 bhp down a hill this steep and then change into a higher gear." At speeds up to 120-130 we went through the streets of Florence, over the great river bridge, broadside across a square, across more tramlines and into the control point. Now Moss had really got the bit between his teeth, nothing was going to stop him winning this race, I felt; he had a rather special look of concentration on his face and I knew that one of his greatest ambitions was to do the section Florence-Bologna in under one hour. This road crosses the heart of the Apennines, by way of the Futa Pass and the Raticosa Pass, and though only just over 60 miles in length it is like a Prescott Hill-Climb all the way. As we got the route card stamped, again without coming to rest, I grabbed the sheet of paper from the Mercedes-Benz man at the control, but before I could read more than that we were still leading, it was torn from my grasp as we accelerated away among the officials. I indicated that we were still leading the race, and by the way Moss left Florence, as though at the start of a Grand Prix, I knew he was out to crack one hour to Bologna, especially as he also looked at his wrist-watch as we left the control. "This is going to be fantastic," I thought, as we screamed up the hills out of Florence, "he is really going to do some nine-tenths plus, motoring" and I took a firm grip of the "struggling bar" between giving him direction signals, keeping the left side of my body as far out of Moss's way as possible, for he was going to need all the room possible for his whirling arms and for stirring the gear-lever about. Up into the mountains we screamed, occasionally passing other cars, such as 1900 Alfa Romeos, Fiats and some small sports cars. Little did we know that we had the race in our pocket, for Taruffi had retired by this time with a broken oil pump and Fangio was stopped in Florence repairing an injection pipe, but though we had overtaken him on the road, we had not seen him, as the car had been hidden by mechanics and officials. All the time I had found it very difficult to take my eyes off the road. I could have easily looked around me, for there was time, but somehow the whole while that Moss was really dicing I felt a hypnotic sensation forcing me to live every inch of the way with him. It was probably this factor that prevented me ever being frightened, for nothing arrived unexpectedly. I was keeping up with him mentally all the way, which I had to do if I wasn't to miss any of our route marking, though physically I had fallen way behind him and I marvelled that anyone could drive so furiously for such a long time, for it was now well into the Sunday afternoon. At the top of the Futa Pass there were enormous crowds all waving excitedly and on numerous occasions Moss nearly lost the car completely as we hit patches of melted tar, coated with oil and rubber from all the other competitors in front of us, and for nearly a mile he had to ease off and drive at a bare eight-tenths, the road was so tricky. Just over the top of the Futa we saw a Mercedes-Benz by the roadside amid a crowd of people; it was 704, young Hans Herrmann, and though we could not see him, we waved. The car looked undamaged so we assumed he was all right.

Now we simply had to get to Brescia first, I thought, we mustn't let Taruffi beat us, still having no idea that he had retired. On we went, up and over the Raticosa Pass, plunging down the other side, in one long series of slides that to me felt completely uncontrolled but to Moss were obviously intentional. However, there was one particular one which was not intentional and by sheer good fortune the stone parapet on the outside of the corner stepped back just in time, and caused us to make rude faces at each other. On a wall someone had painted "Viva Perdisa, viva Maserati" and as we went past in a long controlled slide, we spontaneously both gave it the victory sign, and had a quiet chuckle between ourselves, in the cramped and confined space of our travelling hothouse and bath of filth and perspiration. On another part of the Raticosa amid great crowds of people we saw an enormous fat man in the road, leaping up and down with delight; it was the happy bodybuilder of the Maserati racing department, a good friend of Stirling's, and we waved back to him.

Down off the mountains we raced, into the broiling heat of the afternoon, into Bologna, along the dusty tramlined road, with hordes of spectators on both sides, but here beautifully controlled, so that we went into Bologna at close on 150 mph and down to the control point, Moss doing a superb bit of braking judgment even at this late stage in the race, and in spite of brakes that were beginning to show signs of the terrific thrashing they had been receiving. Here we had the steering column disc punched again and the card stamped, and with another Grand Prix start we were away through the streets of Bologna so quickly that I didn't get the vital news sheet from our depot. Now we had no idea of where we lay in the race, or what had happened to our rivals, but we knew we had crossed the mountains in 1 hr. 1 min., and were so far ahead of Marzotto's record that it seemed impossible. The hard part was now over, but Moss did not relax, for it had now occurred to him that it was possible to get back to Brescia in the round 10 hours, which would make the race average 100 mph. Up the long fast straights through Modena, Reggio Emilia and Parma we went, not wasting a second anywhere, cruising at a continuous 170, cutting off only where I indicated corners, or bumpy hill-brows. Looking up I suddenly realized that we were overtaking an airplane, and then I knew I was living in the realms of fantasy, and when we caught and passed a second one my brain began to boggle at the sustained speed. They were flying at about 300 feet, filming our progress, and it must have looked most impressive, especially as we dropped back by going round the Fidenza by-pass, only to catch up again on the main road. This really was pure speed, the car was going perfectly and reaching 7,600 rpm in fifth gear in places, which was as honest a 170 plus as I'd care to argue about. Going into Piacenza where the road doubles back towards Mantova we passed a 2CV Citroen bowling along merrily, having left Brescia the night before, and then we saw a 2-liter Maserati ahead which shook us perceptibly, for we thought we had passed them all long ago. It was number 621, Francesco Giardini, and appreciating just how fast he must have driven to reach this point before us, we gave him a salutary wave as we roared past, leaving Piacenza behind us. More important was the fact that we were leaving the sun behind us, for nice though it was to have dry roads to race on, the blazing sun had made visibility for both of us very tiring. Through Cremona we went without relaxing and now we were on the last leg of the course, there being a special prize and the Nuvolari Cup for the fastest speed from Cremona to Brescia. Although the road lay straight for most of the way, there were more than six villages to traverse, as well as the final route card stamp to get in the town of Mantova. In one village, less than 50 miles from the finish, we had an enormous slide on some melted tar and for a moment I thought we would hit a concrete wall, but with that absurdly calm manner of his, Moss tweaked the wheel this way and that, and caught the car just in time, and with his foot hard down we

65

went on our way as if nothing had happened. The final miles into Brescia were sheer joy, the engine was singing round on full power, and after we had passed our final direction indication I put my roller-map away and thought "If it blows to pieces now, we can carry it the rest of the way." The last corner into the finishing area was taken in a long slide with the power and noise full on and we crossed the finishing line at well over 100, still not knowing that we had made motor-racing history, but happy and contented at having completed the whole race and done our best.

From the finishing line we drove round to the official garage, where the car had to be parked and Stirling asked "Do you think we've won?" to which I replied, "We must wait for Taruffi to arrive, and we don't know when Fangio got in"—at the garage it was finally impressed upon us that Taruffi was out, Fangio was behind us and we had won. Yes, won the Mille Miglia, achieved the impossible, broken all the records, ruined all the Mille Miglia legends, made history. We clasped each other in delirious joy, and would have wept, but we were too overcome and still finding it hard to believe that we had won. Then we were swept away amid a horde of police and officials, and the ensuing crush amid the wildly enthusiastic crowds was harder to bear than the whole of the 1,000-mile grind we had just completed.

Our total time for the course was 10 hr. 07 min. 48 sec., an average of more than 157 kph (nearly 98 mph) and our average for the 85 miles from Cremona to Brescia had been 123 mph. As we were driven back to our hotel, tired, filthy, oily and covered with dust and dirt, we grinned happily at each other's black face and Stirling said "I'm so happy that we've proved that a Britisher can win the Mille Miglia, and that the legend 'he who leads at Rome never leads at Brescia' is untrue—also, I feel we have made up for the two cars we wrote off in practice," then he gave a chuckle and said "We've rather made a mess of the record, haven't we —sort of spoilt it for anyone else, for there probably won't be another completely dry Mille Miglia for 20 years."

It was with a justified feeling of elation that I lay in a hot bath, for I had had the unique experience of being with Stirling Moss throughout his epic drive, sitting beside him while he worked as I have never seen anyone work before in my life, and harder and longer than I ever thought it possible for a human being to do. It was indeed a unique experience, the greatest experience in the whole of the 22 years during which I have been interested in motor-racing, an experience that was beyond my wildest imagination, with a result that even now I find it extremely hard to believe.

After previous Mille Miglias I have said "he who wins the Mille Miglia is some driver, and the car he uses is some sports car." I now say it again with the certain knowledge that I *know* what I'm talking and writing about this time.

THE OLDEST OF THEM ALL

by W. F. Bradley

This quiet, memorable account of one man's devotion to a motor
car was selected from the book **Motor Racing Memories**, published
in England. Its author, the venerable W. F. Bradley, is a racing journalist of long standing. His career began in 1903, when he followed
the tragic Paris-Madrid race on a bicycle. Over the passing decades,
he has covered most of the great motoring contests, from the Gordon
Bennett Cup races through the Glidden Tours and Grand Prix events.
Here, however, Bradley turns from racing to deal with a humble
man of the cloth, a man devoted to his God and to an ancient
Panhard.

Veterans, like the poor, are always with us. As far back as
1912 Edmund Dangerfield considered that London should
have a veteran car exhibition, which should unite as many
specimens as possible of the first self-propelled vehicles and
present a picture of the romance of motoring. Some of them
had attained the hoary old age of 20 years; generally they
had ceased to run, but, though most of them had very little
mileage to their credit, they were veterans, and the sight of
them only made us prouder of our perfected up-to-date 1912
models—models which, 50 years later, we were seeking
piously to conserve as museum pieces.

It had been ascertained that there was in France a car 21
years old which had been in constant service since the day it
left the maker's hands. Such a car must be secured for the
London museum. The owner was Abbé Gavois, a priest living in the village of Rainneville, a few miles to the northeast of Amiens, and my mission was to persuade him either
to sell his car or to allow it to be sent to London on exhibition.

The Somme region is not one of France's beauty spots.
Rainneville could not be considered picturesque; there was
little in its church to attract the passer-by and its priest

68

could not even be described as passing rich on 40 pounds a year. The presbytery was clean but bare, the main living room having a beaten earth floor; the walls were whitewashed, relieved only by an occasional object of piety, and the shiny black cooking stove in one corner was presided over by a venerable female introduced as "Ma Cousine," who invariably addressed the Priest as "Monsieur le Curé."

According to tradition we were to discuss "business" during lunch, a meal for which "Ma Cousine" had brought out her best linen and had opened a box of sardines to supplement the vegetables, the bread and the cheese which constituted the normal menu, enhanced by a pitcher of local cider. If this Picardy priest lived on a rather lower level than the peasants to whose spiritual needs he administered, he was rich in the possession of ancient cars.

All his affection was focused on a Panhard & Levassor—the sixth car to be produced by that firm—which had left the factory in 1891. Abbé Gavois had an inborn love for mechanics and from the early days had been attracted to the petrol-engined tricycles which preceded cars. On taking up the cure of the village of Rainneville, he had dreamed of the possibility of obtaining a car with which to visit his scattered parishioners. He had no dread of the possible complications of a car; indeed, he was attracted by the problems of maintenance, but the financial problem was one of almost insurmountable difficulty.

"My hope lay in prayer," he explained to me, "and for six months I prayed daily to the Patron Saint that I should be provided with means to secure an automobile. My prayer was answered, for news reached me that M. Buxtorff, Mayor of the town of Troyes, an engineer who had purchased a Panhard & Levassor in 1891, was willing to sell his car at a very low price. He asked 3,000 francs for it, which was very reasonable in view of the thousand francs worth of accessories he had added. But 3,000 francs, *Mon Dieu, c'était une fortune.*"

It was such a tremendous amount of money that the Priest had to decline the offer. Instead of despairing, he continued his prayers until the answer came six weeks later in the form of a letter saying that the Mayor was prepared to dispose of his car for 1,800 francs. A horse and trap would have cost as much and would have been more costly to maintain. With such a scattered parish and having to cover the ten miles into Amiens at frequent intervals, the Abbé decided to buy the Panhard & Levassor.

There is no doubt that it was the sixth car to have been built by the pioneer French firm and, although its twin-cylinder hot tube engine bore the number 77, this is explained by the fact that at the beginning a large number of Panhard & Levassor engines were sold for other than use in a car.

It was decided that the old car should be delivered by rail, and the most convenient station was not Amiens but the small town of Airaines, on National Highway No. 1, a few miles south of Abbeville. Abbé Gavois' début as a motorist was not auspicious. The engine refused to start, and for eight long days it remained stubbornly silent, despite all the efforts at the starting handle and all the ingenuity of the clerical mechanic. Expert advice might have been obtained from Paris, or from Stuttgart, where the engine had been designed, but the Priest had no means of paying for such a luxury. For eight days Abbé Gavois was the laughing-stock of the village of Airaines, the inhabitants of which were not slow in advising the Priest to devote himself to other than mechanical matters. Finally, on the ninth day, the hot tubes burned correctly, the surface carburetor gave the correct mixture, the two cylinders fired evenly and the Priest climbed up behind the tiller and started his journey home at the steady pace of eight miles an hour. The veteran was no toy, it immediately went into daily service and, although its radius of action never exceeded 20 miles, it was invariably used for the varied duties of a Father-Confessor. As it chug-chugged over the Picardy plains, its iron-shod wheels crushing the gravel of by-ways and national highways, it attracted little attention, for it was recognized that it was not dangerous and, as a local poet expressed it, even the hens had time to get out of its way. In the streets of Amiens it was more of a novelty, the boys amusing themselves by running by its side, overtaking it and defiantly waiting its approach, or maliciously hanging on to the folded hood. All of this failed to disturb the equanimity of the priest.

It was soon evident that all attempts to buy the car were doomed to failure. The Abbé, however, appeared willing to lend the car for the exhibition period, providing a substitute was found. Our suggestion that he should take a new 1912 model, with a four-cylinder engine, a four-seater body with folding Cape cart hood, pneumatic tires, oil lamps and acetylene headlights, was turned down with polite firmness.

Such a car was too fast for safety; pneumatic tires would be a source of trouble, if not of danger, the magneto was a bag of mystery and the whole vehicle was too ostentatious for the use of a parish priest. Soon after our arrival, Abbé Gavois had taken us through his shed and shown us his collection of veteran cars, one which today would make any collector envious. Most interesting of all was a Benz with a horizontal single cylinder engine at the rear, built drive, a vertical steering column minus a steering wheel, solid rubber tires at the rear, front wheels intended to receive pneumatics (obviously a transformation) and the skeleton of a two-seater body. Weeks would be necessary to put such a car into running order, even if several essential parts could be obtained, and it had to be ruled out as a substitute. A similar decision had to be taken regarding a motor tricycle.

There remained a car of unknown make, sufficiently slow for safety, but which had the grave defect of having big diameter rear wheels fitted with pneumatic tires, incidentally in a condition quite beyond repair. Tires of this diameter were no longer manufactured, but we felt that they could be made specially and we set about the difficult task of convincing the priest that the pneumatics would not cause him any inconvenience. It was not easy to persuade him that punctures and bursts were not daily occurrences. We quoted our own example of 2,000 miles without a single puncture, and we sometimes drove at the giddy pace of 40 miles an hour. His tires would be new, his speed would be low and he could rely on them giving reliable service during the six weeks they would be on the road. Finally, he consented to lend the car. The Oldest of Them All was packed, sent to London, put on exhibition and then returned to Picardy to continue its daily runs through the little villages entrusted to the care of this kindly and simple priest. For 38 years it continued in service, with no other attention than that given by its owner. It was not insured, for it never caused an accident; it was not registered and carried no number plates, for the French have that happy quality of ignoring a law which has ceased to be useful. Registration was merely adopted as a means of identification, and why identify a car by means of number plates when it was familiar to every policeman and gendarme in the entire district?

The war came and in the turmoil I forgot about Abbé Gavois and his veteran. But with the return of peace, I

71

once more paid a visit to the village of Rainneville, where Abbé Gavois was still carrying on his duties in the same quiet, unobtrusive manner—and his ancient car was still intact and in daily service. The Picardy plains had been the scene of some of the most bitter fighting in the great war and on one occasion Rainneville had been overrun by the invading forces.

"What did you do?" I asked the priest.

"Oh, I just stayed," was the quiet answer. And as if in explanation he added, "You see I am a direct descendant of General Cambronne."

During practically the whole of the war the Somme district was held by British troops. The stubborn peasants refused to be evacuated except by force and claimed the right to cultivate their fields even amongst the field artillery. All the younger priests having been called up for service, additional work fell on Abbé Gavois and his car. If outsiders were not allowed to penetrate this district, the ancient Panhard & Levassor trundled along day after day, minus a pass, minus number plates, sharing the road with guns and supply columns, marching troops and dashing staff cars. Its petrol requirements were so low that it never had any difficulty in securing fuel. Indeed, the British Army almost adopted the old French priest and was always prepared to leave behind a can of petrol if they thought it would be of use.

"Ils étaient gentille," explained the priest. If the soldiers admired the quiet courage of this village priest, they were deeply interested in the veteran car, and captains, majors, colonels and even a general asked to be allowed to ride in it.

"But you must have had some rough times," I insisted.

"Yes," he admitted. "We had an Australian battery in action in the village. Finally the Germans spotted it and sent planes over to bomb it. The havoc was terrible. They are all buried at Rainneville," he added sadly.

In the summer of 1918 the German forces made a last desperate effort to break through the Allied lines and bring the war to a conclusion. It was realized by the Allied command that the fate of Europe depended on the resistance they could offer and every available man was thrown into the firing line. Even General Pershing, who had sought to maintain his forces intact, under American command, on the eastern portion of the line, found it necessary to detach important units and place them under French and

72

British command at this most threatened point of the battle front.

Rainneville was overrun and Amiens was reached. But this success was of short duration, for on July 14th the Allies struck back with force, regaining Rainneville with its priest and its handful of inhabitants, and continued with increasing pressure to drive the enemy northwards and eastwards, until victory came four months later.

A competition was opened for the oldest car having been maintained in regular service from the time it left the maker's hands. There were older cars than the Panhard & Levassor, but they had all been placed in retirement; if they came out, it was merely for a demonstration run; some of them were quite incapable of travelling under their own power.

To his surprise and embarrassment, Abbé Gavois found himself a prominent figure and his old car an object of respect and admiration. Now, it was insisted, he must part with it and as its sale involved a substantial amount of money which could be devoted to charity, the Abbé consented, after long and serious thought and prayer.

"You must have had some adventures during the 37 years this car has been in service," we suggested.

"Well, just a few over such a long period and a distance of more than 150,000 miles. But I am proud to say that it never caused a serious accident. On one occasion a carter was inattentive and could not control his horse when it took fright at the smell of the car. The cart was overturned, but nobody was hurt. On one occasion I escaped what might have been a serious accident, for while I was travelling downhill at more than ten miles an hour, the steering gear became ineffective. One of the clevis pins, instead of being held by a nut, was merely secured by a split pin. This wore and dropped out, leaving me without any control over the car. Fortunately I was able to stop before any damage was done. Many have scoffed at my veteran, but ridicule never hurt anybody and it is better to have caused laughter than anger and tears."

The last journey should be a return to Paris and the factory in which the car had been produced in 1891. "No, it must not be dishonored by being put on the train. It was old, but it was reliable," maintained the priest, "and it must cover the 80-odd miles under its own power and in one day."

Except for its journey to London by train and boat, the

Veteran had never left the Somme plains during the years it had been in the Abbé's possession and it had rarely been more than 20 miles from its home. Hills had to be encountered on the road to Paris and there was an intensity of traffic unknown in the days of its youth. But the Oldest of Them All was capable of facing even these conditions. Indeed, it was a matter of pride that it should accomplish this journey unaided after the honors which had been bestowed on it in a banquet at Amiens, attended by the Préfet in person, by a General and by the President of the Automobile Club of France.

Enthusiasm increased as the veteran approached Paris until, after it had passed through the old gates and entered the Avenue de la Grande Armée, the crowd insisted on pushing the car up the slight rise. The Priest protested seriously, for this overflowing enthusiasm was an implication of feebleness on the part of his faithful companion. Lost in the crowd surrounding it, the Panhard chugged round the magnificent Arc de Triomph and entered the gentle downgrade of the Champs Elysées, leading to the Place de la Concorde. That beautiful avenue has been the scene of many a magnificent cavalcade, but never one so human, so powerfully simple and moving as that of the village priest presenting the Oldest of Them All to the authorities gathered in front of the Automobile Club.

DARK INHERITANCE

by Erwin C. Lessner

This is the story of a man with courage and ambition—two qualities on the wane at this mid-point of the 20th century. He did what he did because he had to. An inner flame burned, and had it not been released, it surely would have ignited the soul of Pierre Levegh. To want as he wanted, to fight as he fought, are the marks of the individual, uncommon man. So, although he ended tragically, it was probably inevitable for he was following that inner flame.

Among racing drivers of all nations, Pierre Levegh, of France, was a remarkable man. He could drive a car over road and track as a violinist guides his bow. He had stamina, intelligence, willpower, dedication and a flair for engineering perfection which enabled him to squeeze an additional bit of performance out of the best automobiles of his time.

He was by no means the greatest of drivers. He held no titles or championships; he raced but seldom. In a sport populated by many virtuosos, Levegh merely was an excellent driver. In one respect, however, he was unique: he had been raised and deliberately groomed for his uncommon occupation. Ever since he could remember, his family had told him that racing was his true vocation, his duty to his clan.

The Leveghs had an unusual family hero. In the pioneer era of automobile racing in Europe, an early Levegh had won a number of road races in Mors cars. The first Levegh remained a popular hero in France for several racing seasons beginning in 1898—but then the cheers faded away. Other names—Jenatzy, De Knyff, Lancia, Nazzaro—crowded the sports pages.

The Levegh family kept the memory of the cheers like flowers in an herbarium. There was no other male Levegh to carry on the family tradition—not until the famous driver's sister, a Madame Bouillin, had a son, Pierre.

Born several years after his uncle's retirement, little Pierre Bouillin was told the sagas of motor racing together with his first nursery rhymes. At an age when other boys concentrate on cops and robbers, he was made aware of his great life's mission: to revive the exalted glory of the family and carry it to immortality on the race track.

There was no family car for Pierre to sit in and play at racing; cars were a luxury in pre-World-War-I France. Pierre, however, had the cars of his imagination and his family was always ready to hear him tell of his dreamed exploits in races of fantasy. Eventually, a family palaver decided that the boy should adopt the name of his uncle. Pierre Bouillin legally became Pierre Levegh.

It was difficult to enter the racing profession in a France digging out from the debris of the first World War. Established makers of racing cars relied on drivers whose popularity had survived the holocaust. New talent had to struggle its way up as relief men, as drivers of reserve cars and in smaller contests in which the stars did not care to stake their reputations. And a boy just out of high school was not even considered new talent.

After writing endless applications without success, Pierre came to realize that his new and famous name did not impress car makers. He started, instead, as an apprentice at a small private garage—but he was operating a broom not a steering wheel.

Unknown then to young Levegh, born Bouillin, two men important to automobile racing held a meeting one day in 1922—a meeting that would affect his entire life. While Pierre labored, French automobile expert and racing fan, George Durant, and Charles Faroux, dean of French automobile writers, conceived a new type of competition: an endurance test for production cars. It was known as the 24 Hours of Le Mans, and the first race was held in May of 1923. The winner would be the car which covered the greatest distance in 24 hours. The site of the race was a road circuit near the ancient city of Le Mans.

Repair-shop apprentice Pierre Levegh was among the 100,-000 spectators who saw two Frenchmen, André Lagache and René Leonard, win the first Le Mans race. Then and there Pierre decided that this was the greatest automotive contest of all times. The same was to be said of Le Mans by other observers at other times. Among other annual events, its fame grew. It came to be called the Queen of

Races. To Pierre Levegh, however, it was, from the first, the Only Race.

Seldom in the history of sport has a venture been more thoroughly prepared, or more fanatically pursued. Levegh started his preparations not by driving but by doing garage and repair work. He realized that to win at Le Mans required an intimate knowledge of machinery.

As a mechanic, Levegh soon became the Sunday speeder's best helper. He had a way with automobiles. He came to understand every mood of an engine, every trick of brakes and transmissions. He could coax machines into delivering unexpected bits of extra performance. Sly tricks—polishing of carburetor barrels, manipulations of valves, a touch on the ignition—might make a car do 51 mph instead of 49.

Word of Levegh's talent got around. He acquired a growing and faithful clientele and had constant offers of better jobs. Grudging competitors called him shrewd. But he was not really shrewd. He just wanted to give every automobile, however modest, the sort of treatment he would give his own future automobile at Le Mans. When testing other people's unspectacular cars, he drove them Le Mans style. He could literally throw a rickety small sedan into a turn as if it were a low-slung sports car and come out whole and fast.

The Le Mans race was held in June, in the period of longest daylight. Every June for years, Levegh went to Le Mans to see other drivers race and win. He came to learn and to know every yard of the road, every intricacy of its turns and grades. He saw the most famous racers on the finest sports cars attack the circuit. He remembered their every trick and pitfall and he could have steered over the course blindfolded.

For 12 years, between 1924 and 1935, no French car won the great prize. While Britishers and Italians prevailed, Pierre Levegh's strange inner fire was fanned by a new resolve: to restore not only his family's, but also his country's glory.

Yet, as the years passed, Levegh's excellent reputation as a master tuner and test driver brought no offers to pilot a car at Le Mans. He entered a few rallies and, despite unspectacular cars (some of them owned by his customers) he awed other competitors by his dash and daring.

Next, he tried to ingratiate French automobile makers in order to make them, at long last, put him to the test for

Le Mans. Manufacturers notice those who sell their goods and Levegh was a good salesman. Customers liked him. He knew what he was talking about and he looked the part: tall, sturdy, sharp-featured, radiating knowledge and self-assertion. Soon, the makers of Talbot automobiles became acquainted with Levegh and inevitably, learned of his burning ambition. On a hunch and a gamble, Talbot's chief designer, Antoine Lago, offered Levegh his first opportunity to drive in the Queen of Races. It was 1938. Levegh had been waiting for 15 years.

The "great opportunity" was actually less than great, however. Lago wanted a relief driver for Jean Trévoux, an old and not strictly lucky hand at Le Mans. Trévoux had tried the 24 Hours three times since 1932, with a record of one mechanical failure, one accident and one seventh place. But Lago considered him a good driver and gave him the fifth car in the Talbot team of six. Levegh made his debut then as a second-string driver on a fifth-string car. In the race, the car broke down before Levegh even took the wheel.

This anti-climax to a life of toil and longing might have crushed another man, but not Levegh. He erased the memory of 1938 from his mind, and in 1939 made his annual trip to Le Mans as a spectator to watch Jean-Pierre Wimille and Pierre Veyron drive a Bugatti to victory. It was a splendid ride, yet there was nothing, Levegh thought, in the performance that he could not have done at least as well. This conviction strengthened his iron resolve to reach the lifelong goal.

When 1940 came, however, war had returned to Europe and for a full decade there was no race at Le Mans. Levegh, like every other good patriot, smarted under the military disaster of France. He also had a special grievance: the Germans, who had never scored in the 24 Hours, razed and bulldozed the course establishments at Le Mans. They turned the track into a fighter base and used the roads as runways. In turn, Allied bombers plastered the place. When the invaders finally left, after four years of occupation, they destroyed everything. Le Mans reverted into a dullish provincial town of 120,000, and in its surroundings nothing moved faster than a few rickety cars, asthmatic trucks and horse-drawn wagons. To Pierre Levegh, older now and saddened, Le Mans was his Sleeping Beauty.

Sleeping Beauty awoke in 1949, however, and Pierre Levegh again was a spectator. The reawakened Le Mans was a parade of stars. Juan Manuel Fangio, Froilan Gonzales, René

Dreyfus, Luigi Chinetti, Louis Chiron, Raymond Sommer, were among the celebrities who graced the big show. Ferrari, Jaguar, Bentley, Aston Martin bowed in the cast of cars.

Levegh viewed men and machines without frustration. He was now well in his forties, but he knew that at Le Mans age was no serious handicap: experience was more important than youthful tempestuousness. Petite, dark-haired Madame Levegh shared her husband's confidence that a new chance would come. It did—in 1951.

Despite the fact that the Talbot people would not allow Levegh to apply his own wizardry to the preparing of the car, they nevertheless assigned him a big 4½-liter automobile in factory tune. It was not what Levegh would have wanted, but it was a ride. After all, he had been waiting 28 years.

Talbot entered six cars in 1951 and again Levegh ranked fifth. He tested his car in practice. It did 150 on straightaways, but Ferraris were clocked at 160 and Jaguars at nearly 170. More annoying, Levegh's car was inferior to at least three other Talbots in the team. Tony Lago had reserved better machines for the more famous drivers. Levegh shrugged.

Bad odds could not discourage a man who had gone through so much. With co-driver René Marchand, Levegh gave a good account of himself, finishing fourth at an average speed of 89 mph for 24 hours.

Newspapers gave Levegh-Marchand the honorable-mention treatment. Levegh ignored it. After half a lifetime he had at last and at least driven in his Queen of Races. To have finished at all was a victory—but not enough of a victory for Pierre Levegh. He had tasted blood and he wanted more. He would try again.

Lago had believed in him, so he would remain faithful to Talbot cars—but if Talbot insisted that factory-owned cars must be factory-prepared, he would buy his own car for the 1952 race and adapt it as he pleased. All he wanted was early delivery of a new model.

The car was delivered in November 1951. It carried a price tag of nearly four million francs, the equivalent of $10,000. It would have been the rave of showrooms. Mechanically, however, it did not essentially differ from its 1951 predecessor.

Levegh called in his old collaborators. No more expert a team of experimenters and tinkerers could have been assembled anywhere and no finer guiding brain and co-ordinator could have been found than Levegh himself. He was by now a man possessed, on the threshold of triumph. The team did not leave a single part of the car in its place. Regulations permitted a very slight increase of piston displacement. They went to the strict limit, increased engine compression and labored hard on the three carburetors. The improved engine gave the Talbot the extra acceleration for which drivers have been clamoring since the day of the first Levegh.

The gas tank was a major problem on Le Mans cars. Regulations set the minimum interval between refueling at 25 laps (about 210 miles). The Talbot had a 40 gallon tank which gave it a basic range of 300 miles. Levegh thought that 330 would be safer, so a new tank containing 44 gallons was built in. This in turn caused an increase in weight. Since every ounce might reduce speed by one yard per hour and the loss of 24 yards could decide the issue, weight had to be saved on the body. Under the strict Le Mans rules, cars had to carry "touring body work" and to have "in good operating order and properly attached throughout the race, doors, windshields, fenders, hood, side and rear lamps, means of audible warning, and rear windows." Also, there had to be plenty of room for tools and spares for only those tools and spares carried aboard car at the start could be used during the race.

Levegh went to work on a completely new body. When the task was completed, the all-aluminum structure weighed a mere 36½ lbs.

Work had been going on for two months when the tinkerers remembered that wiring trouble had cost many a Le Mans competitor precious minutes in the past. Levegh ordered a complete second set of wiring to be installed.

Five thousand expensive man hours went into the adaptation and reconstruction of Levegh's 1952 car. His total investment was then nearly six million francs. A Frenchman might invest six million francs in a solid business venture and live happily ever after, but not so Levegh. For him there could be no more important investment than the one he had made in the mighty Talbot. Rationally speaking, the car was a travesty of an investment. If it won the great prize in addition to all hourly bonuses, Levegh could collect two million francs at the most. But this man did not have the mind of a shop-keeper. He had only the blindness of devotion. Madame Levegh agreed with her Pierre, as always. She did not mind the huge expense: they had no children.

Race day, June 14, 1952, was a crisp and clear Saturday. More than 250,000 people lined the eight-mile irregularly shaped course. At the main public enclosures, at Tertre Rouge, near Les Esses, crowds of more than 100,000 per square mile set up camps which ancient American Indians would have considered extravagantly colorful. They unpacked prodigal quantities of food and wine, while in the grandstands, box-seat customers and distinguished holders of passes sat in elegance.

The start was set for 4 P.M. By 3:30, the excited prattle of the crowd all but drowned out the thunder of passing aircraft and the savage growl of high-compression car engines. Only grandstand dwellers and privileged campers on the western fringe of the Tertre Rouge enclosure had a view of the start and finish line. Everywhere else, in the thin groves of Les Esses, at White House corner to the north, on the undulating stretch between the bridge east of Tertre Rouge and the rectangular turn of Mulsanne, people read programs and imagined the great lineup.

Fifty-nine cars stood in a sharp angle to the road, ready to run round and round, counter-clockwise until 4 P.M. Sunday —or as long as they might last. Twenty-one cars in the array were French: big Talbots, compact high-powered Gordinis; light Dyna Panhards, Peugeots, Renaults, and Simcas. The French loved them all. Eighteen cars were from Britain: sturdy Allards, sleek Aston Martins, massive Jaguars, sporty Frazer-Nashes, and less formidable-looking Nash-Healeys, Jowett Jupiters, and Morgans. The crowd respected them, in particular the Jaguars. Italy had an expeditionary force of nine: roaring Ferraris, sure-wheeled Lancias, and novel Oscas. The Italians were Latin cousins and the French had a soft spot for noisy Latin antics of all varieties. The Americans were here with three mighty Cunninghams, biggest of the lot. The French crowd wished the list of starters would end there, but there were six more cars: the Germans had come down across the Rhine again, this time to conquer the 24 Hours. Their tools were varied: Mercedes-Benz latest super sports models, with doors opening like gull wings; and the fabulous little Porsche cars.

At 3:45, the drivers emerged from their pits. They wore brassards of brightly colored cloth: red for main drivers, green for relief drivers, blue for the reserve-men. Usually, main drivers opened the battle to pilot their cars into good positions. Alberto Ascari, World Champion, was the star of stars. There were Le Mans winners of the past: Luigi

Chinetti, Louis Rosier, Eugene Chaboud. There was also Stirling Moss who held the lap record of 105 mph. There was applause for Luigi Billoresi, the middle-aged Italian acrobat of the steering wheel: for Robert Manzon and for Jean Behra, and for illustrious newcomers Duane Carter, fourth at Indianapolis in 1952, and John Fitch, the up-and-coming American. Masses stared in silence at the smart German successors to the swastika era, Karl Kling and Hermann Lang.

But only a few stared at Pierre Levegh, the tall man in light overalls, who would drive Number Eight. No reason to stare at him. He was not a star, not even a familiar name. Levegh himself felt good, tense and confident, and he gave little thought to favorites or celebrities or the stares of the crowd. This was *his* day. He turned and smiled at his wife. She smiled back, as confident as her husband.

Nervous pit mechanics called out minutes, then seconds. Ten, nine, eight, seven, six, five, four, three, two . . . ONE —GO! Fifty-seven men ran across the road toward their automobiles.

Levegh galloped across the road and was off in one of the most spectacular starts, but the crowd still hardly noticed him. Nevertheless, he had his own carefully considered plan and he would stick to it. He knew that his Talbot was not as fast as the Ferraris and the Jaguars, yet faster than the other Talbots. He noticed also that it was faster than the Mercedes-Benz. He steered it safely, regularly.

In the early stages of the race, Le Mans crowds are exclusively interested in first position. Later, as the field thins and changes occur along the line, they study signboards as if they were strategic maps in a war. In 1952, the field thinned rapidly. The Jaguars' radiators caused trouble. Ferrari engines were too powerful for their clutches. Duane Carter's Cunningham was a casualty. One hour after sunset, the dead car park had 17 occupants. Gordini still held the lead. Levegh, driving with chronometric regularity, averaging 100 mph was second. He felt elated and confident.

With the coming of night the course became a fast white way. Acres of scoreboards and advertising displays were illuminated by dazzling reflectors. 10 P.M., 11 P.M. The whining of wheels, the roar of engines, the background of snoring as the first shift of sleepers dozed off on grandstands and enclosures. On most cars relief drivers were now in action. The track had turned into a rack: *La Ronde Impitoyable*—The Pitiless Round—as it was called. Turning a course 100,

200, close to 300 times is like sitting in front of a screen on which the same motion picture turns up every five minutes, day and night in monotonous succession. The visual ordeal is difficult to bear. The driver can concentrate on nothing but the phantom screen of the road, with occasional glances at the instrument panel and the signals at his pit. There is a strong temptation to strain the machine to get it over with: there is a constant fight against monotony and fatigue and against the engine's perilous insensitivity.

When Levegh made his third fuel stop, he found his co-driver Marchand set to take over, but waved him off. He still had a fundamental job to do: take the lead at the half-way mark and keep dangerous rivals at a safe distance. He also had a personal dragon to slay: the 24 Hours.

The Gordini had lapped him but Levegh did not consider the Gordini dangerous. A signal indicated that the true menace, Mercedes-Benz, was more than two laps behind him.

Midnight! The Gordini still in front.

3 A.M. The Gordini sputtered. Ignition trouble. Levegh overtook the limping car near the grandstand. The fundamental job was done. Levegh was in first place after 11 consecutive hours of driving without relief.

He could have relaxed and rested then but his mind did not properly conceive this thought. He was getting weary. Weariness produces a state of obstinacy or apathy. By nature not a yielding man, Levegh grew extremely obstinate. "I must win," he said to himself. The emphasis was on *I*. Co-driver Marchand had no part in his plans. After 29 years, Pierre Levegh was in headlong pursuit of his dragon.

At halftime, sleepers rose, everybody checked signal boards. Levegh, in first place, had covered 142 laps, two Mercedes-Benz 138, another Talbot, an Aston Martin, an Allard and a struggling Ferrari had made 132, the Cunningham 126.

Fog, the traditional plague of Le Mans' small hours, closed in. Through the thin wisps, 250,000 pairs of eyes now looked for Levegh's Number Eight. 250,000 people talked about Levegh, cheered him, and in the dawn hours began to build him into a national hero. Levegh could not know what went on along the track, but he knew what went on *on* it. He was set to win. The Levegh tradition was about to be restored. Twelve more hours and he would have achieved what he had longed to do for nearly 30 years.

At the pit, Mrs. Levegh leaned over the wall, affectionately peering into the pale light to catch a glimpse of her husband's face. Wasn't he tired? Wasn't it time for him to cede the wheel to Marchand? For a few laps at least?

Number Eight roared past. The driver's face was hardly visible. The wife and her husband's relief driver exchanged glances. A graying pitman grumbled. Levegh was a fool not to stop—but then he was due for refueling soon. Probably he did not want to make an extra stop.

Only 31 cars were still in the race. The two Mercedes were running second and third with perfect regularity although four laps behind Levegh. Racing Manager Alfred Neubauer, accomplished racing strategist and disciplinarian, was in total charge. Everything in his pits was done in step; all work was done in swift, cadenced motions, and the mechanics slept in formation. German drill had outlived both the Second and the Third Reich and Herr Neubauer's word was law. No questions were asked when he ordered *his* drivers in for relief. Crouched on a high stool, his 300 pounds towered over his white-clad crew. The German position seemed difficult. Four laps are not easily made up unless the leader runs into trouble. Neubauer watched, sharp-eyed and sharp-eared. He would issue orders in time.

But nobody could order Pierre Levegh to cede the wheel. And when Marchand pleaded with him at the next pit stop, Levegh absent-mindedly munched an orange and took off after refueling.

As the sun rose, the Talbot engine sounded perfect and the weary Levegh drove with a perfection that blended acrobatics and scholarship. "Levegh rides his car like a thoroughbred horse," somebody said. The slogan was taken up by the enthusiastic crowd. They could not know that the lone driver was beginning to act like an automaton.

As morning grew bright, Number Eight kept turning the Pitiless Round to a quarter-million French cheers. Levegh! Levegh! 250,000 throats turned hoarse with the name. The audience saw the main driver's red brassard. "So Levegh is doing it all himself!" Only a few men had tried it before, but none had succeeded. More hurrahs for Levegh, then, who would win alone.

As he passed his pit again, he leaned slightly to the right. His wife saw his sagging chin. So did the chief mechanic and Marchand. They knew what it meant. Levegh could not keep on rolling forever. He would have to cede the wheel for a time at least. He could be back in the driver's seat for the finish. He shouldn't jeopardize his victory!

Like a dead man at the wheel, Levegh came in for refueling at mid morning. His mental processes were then reduced to a point at which he had practically lost the faculty of reasoning and would keep switching, stepping and turning until he would collapse. When Marchand made a desperate attempt to hop into the car to take over, the crazed driver blocked his way and was off, alone. An attempt by Madame Levegh to feed her husband drugs failed. He gulped some mineral water but spit the pills.

By midday, with four hours remaining, 19 cars were left and Number Eight miles ahead. The two Mercedes were next. But Herr Neubauer still did not issue emergency orders. His pit was in sight of Levegh's and the bulky commander-in-chief of the German expeditionary force had had a close look at the Frenchman at each refuel stop. He expected him neither to last to the end nor to cede the wheel.

Four more hours. One more refueling stop. Levegh's complexion had turned greenish, his eyes glassy, his hands jittery. Violent stomach pain caused by vertigo, distorted his features. He could not even close his mouth. But he did not get up from his seat behind the big Talbot wheel. Marchand shook him, shouted at him, all to no avail. Sagging, hate gleaming dully in his eyes, Levegh prevented the other man from squeezing in at his side. Madame Levegh talked to her husband: he did not understand her pleading words and his glazed eyes did not register her picture. An old friend and sports writer had been waiting at the pits; Levegh did not recognize him. Mechanics tried to communicate with Levegh but he did not notice them.

Finally, its tanks filled and sealed, the Talbot rolled again. The crowd cheered. Mrs. Levegh had tears in her eyes. Marchand and the pit crew sat in dispirited silence.

Three hours to go. Number Eight carried on, the driver's head hanging sideways.

Two hours to go. Number Eight far out in front, Levegh now a faltering robot.

One more hour. The Talbot had held an average of almost 100 mph. An average of 80 during the last hour would be ample to secure victory. A pitman chalked a slowdown signal on a board. But the faltering robot could not read.

Fifty minutes, 40 minutes. The Talbot was 25 whole miles ahead of one Mercedes and 35 ahead of the other. A leisurely average of 60 mph would win it all. But Levegh did not slow down.

Another lap. The Lang-Reiss Mercedes raced past the grandstand. Everybody waited for Levegh. But for the first time in over 23 hours, there was no sign of him. Silence settled on the grandstand.

Then a loudspeaker blared: "Number Eight, Pierre Levegh, broken down between Arnage and White House."

An official car brought Levegh to his pit, almost lifeless. For two hours he lay in a corner vomiting, then recovered sufficiently to weep in the embrace of his disconsolate wife. He was practically unconscious when the results were announced: Mercedes-Benz first and second. The crowd was in such angry mood that the racing committee did not dare have the German anthem played.

Later, much later, the stewards announced the mechanical reason for Levegh's breakdown: broken crankshaft. The human reason was the true one, however. The weary man, in trying to shift from fourth into third, had dazedly shoved the lever toward first instead. The odds were a thousand to one that he could not get into first at such high speed, but he succeeded, pushing the engine to revolutions which no crankshaft could stand.

For Levegh, the blow of 1952 was infinitely worse than that of 1938. There seemed now to be no possibility of resuming the pursuit of the dragon. He could not afford to spend another six million francs on a car and his physical condition would hardly be as good. No comfort came from the public. The 250,000 did not sympathize with their erstwhile hero but resented his defaulting them. Charles Faroux commented: "The laws of sports are harsh and immutable. You have got to run all the way in order to win. We may be sorry for Levegh and his wonderful effort, but Mercedes-Benz met the essential requirements by driving a steady, well-controlled race from start to finish."

To Levegh, however, abandonment of his goal to win Le Mans would have been abandonment of all he stood for. Lago promised him another car for 1953. It would be a plain factory model with improved streamlining.

The racing committee amended the terms of the 24 Hours to the effect that henceforth no man was permitted to drive more than 18 hours.

Levegh's ride of 1953 did not hold public interest. He seemed a has-been who never quite had been. His Talbot was best among the French cars. Fourteen others, however, finished ahead of him.

As always after races, he returned to his regular business of tuning, repairing, selling automobiles—364 busy days which, to him, were but so many days of impatient waiting.

In 1954 Talbot invested one more car in Pierre Levegh's heart-rending venture. For several hours he was first among the French, trailing seven foreign cars. Then he struck a bank close to the spot where tragedy had struck him in 1952. The Talbot was damaged beyond repair.

Finally, a year later, on Saturday, June 11, 1955, while the same annual crowd gathered around the Pitiless Round, Mercedes-Benz, Ferrari and Jaguar battled for the prize of Le Mans. In the evening hours three cars approached the short straightaway behind the right hand turn near Les Esses: a Jaguar passed an Austin-Healey as Mercedes Number 20 roared into the slot. A second later, the Jaguar was out in the clear, the Austin-Healey veered, and Number 20 erupted into the packed humanity bordering the course.

Those who lived to tell remembered no more than a bright flash, an infernal roar, and a shower of dark objects hitting people with the sound and impact of cannon balls. The enclosure turned into a red-and-dark sea of maimed bodies. Men, women and children were smashed, burned, and decapitated by murderous debris. Eighty-three perished instantly or were soon dead. It was the worst disaster in racing history.

The driver of Mercedes Number 20 probably died before he realized what disaster had befallen his countrymen. For *his* countrymen they were. He was Pierre Levegh.

The ardent French patriot, faithful adherent to Talbot and Lago, rugged individualist, had, in 1955, accepted an offer by Neubauer, the man who thought even better of Levegh than Levegh's own countrymen. In the pursuit of his personal dragon, Pierre Levegh was ready to make concessions, even to drive a German car, rather than forego his design. He wanted to show the world that he could set a mark at Le Mans that would always be remembered. Through no fault of his own he succeeded.

AUSTRALIA'S MAD REDEX TRIAL

by Jeff Carter

Track and circuit racing form only a part of automotive competition. Hillclimbs, Gymkanas, timed acceleration runs, rallies, and trials also occupy their rightful place in the sport. In America, the rally is probably the most popular form of competition, since the wife or girl friend may be taken along to do her navigational part toward a trophy. But the major rallies, the famed Monte Carlo and Alpine runs in Europe, are less of a lark, demanding a fantastic degree of driving skill, navigational expertise, and just plain luck. Yet, to our minds, even these rigorous events must bow to the wildest, woolliest motoring contest of them all—the Redex!

". . . Redex Trial drivers are nothing but inhuman madmen. The wicked and scandalous way speeding drivers kill and maim kangaroos saddens me. I would like to stop this mad thing and have every speeding and dangerous driver clapped in jail . . ."

This outraged cry was voiced by the president of Australia's Society for the Prevention of Cruelty to Animals when competitors in the world's toughest and longest car trial were reported to have run down hundreds of kangaroos in one day. A Sydney driver in a Ford Customline claimed he had struck 28 animals in 170 miles. Australia's car trials idol and hot favorite to win the Redex, Eric Nelson, hit a 7-ft. high kangaroo while travelling at speed in his Standard Vanguard Spacemaster and wrecked the vehicle. The rest of the 184 competing cars also took their toll.

The massacre occurred during the 21-day, 10,533 mile long Redex Car Trial around wild and woolly outback Australia, where white settlements are few and far between and wild blacks, buffalo, crocodiles and kangaroos roam as freely as they did in the stone age.

And the roads . . . most of them are little more than

tracks, and they pass through some of the roughest, remotest, uncivilized wasteland in the world. When it rains, the "roads" become near-impassable bogs, with treacherous, bridgeless creek and river crossings every few miles. When it doesn't rain, the merciless Centralian sun sucks up every drop of water for hundreds of miles, creating desert conditions as formidable as the world's worst.

During the Trial, crocodiles attacked a contestant's car that stalled in a deep river crossing, while angry natives threatened crews of wrecked vehicles on the border of the aboriginal reserve in Arnhem Land, near Darwin, Australia's north-west port. Of the 184 cars that started in the 1955 Redex Trial, only 57 limped across the finishing line, and of these, 20 or more were thoroughly "clapped"—fit only for the junk yard.

Why do drivers wreck their cars each year in the Around Australia Redex Trial?

For money—and, perhaps, glory.

More than 20,000 dollars, in the form of prize-money, comes the way of leading place-getters, while at least as much again is paid to the winners by auto-accessories manufacturers in return for testimonials praising their product. And that sort of money, in Australia, is not regarded as hay. It is customary, too, for the winner of the Trial to be presented with a brand new vehicle by the manufacturers of the car he drove to victory.

A wide variety of cars enter the Redex lists each year, including American Fords, Plymouths, Hudsons, Dodges, Chevrolets and Studebakers. But the bulk of the cars are the lighter European types: Peugeot, Volkswagen, Skoda, Vanguard, Morris, Renault, Hillman, Fiat and Australia's own car, the Holden.

These lighter, shorter, high-road-clearance vehicles are more easily dragged from bogs and don't sink so readily in sand and bulldust. They have a better chance, too, of negotiating steep V creek crossings, where longer cars smash front and rear fenders simultaneously on opposing angles of road.

The first Redex (the Trial is an annual event), held in 1953, was won by a Peugeot. In 1954, the event went to a 1948 Ford V-8.

No car owner in a sound state of mind would endeavor to even FOLLOW the tortuous, lonely and dangerous route taken by the Redex contestants, much less try to maintain the high average speeds expected between "control points" in the Trial. For example, on one 62-mile horror stretch near Mount Isa, in the tropical state of Queensland, where the road consists of poorly defined wheel tracks over rugged, rock-strewn, thickly-bushed hills, there are 58 creekbed crossings through running streams. The average speed required for this section was 41 mph. A route survey car had not been able to better 12 mph before the Trial.

But the ultimate place-getters were only four minutes late getting through! How come? Uncanny driving skill, product of years of outback "trials" experience enabled crack professional drivers to best such horror stretches—plus an occasional smile from Lady Luck.

Thirty or more of Australia's leading competition drivers took part in the '55 Redex, but smashes with kangaroos, buffaloes, wild donkeys and camels, trees, ant hills, boulders and other competitors, loss of direction (in central Australia, navigation is done by compass) and other strokes of bad luck put many of them out of the running. Most novice drivers found the going too rough, and their abandoned vehicles littered the 10,533-mile route. Many crashed badly at speed and were hospitalized.

Many of the nation's star drivers suffered badly at the hands of Lady Luck, to the disappointment of fans who turned up at unexpected places along the route to cheer their favorites. Veteran trials man Peter Antill, of Sydney, stopped his Plymouth to open the Border Gate in a rabbit-proof fence that separates South from West Australia. It was night, pitch black. Another contestant, driving at 70 mph with damaged, flickering headlights, crashed into the rear of Antill's car. The driver and navigator of the second car were injured, but their safety belts, ripped from the floor by the impact, saved them from death.

Another favorite for the event, Jack "Gelignite" Murray, who won in 1954 with a Ford V-8, also suffered a string of mishaps. He earned his name, incidentally, through his habit of throwing lighted sticks of dynamite from his car when passing through the main streets of quiet country towns at night. Police arrested him for this, so this year he threw colored balloons to children who had gathered to cheer him through their towns, frightened others by wearing an ape face mask. Jack "got lost" on one outback stretch and forfeited points. Later he blew two tires in quick succession and fell further back. Finally his car bogged down irrevocably only 200 miles from the finishing line and he withdrew from the Trial.

Another "ace" competitor and idol of the crowds, Keith Thallon, was among the leaders until the alpine section, in Victoria's snow country. Four hundred miles from "home" he left the road on a hairpin bend, rolled his car end-over-end three times into a ravine.

Mishaps to other competitors throughout the trial were frequent and varied. A Peugeot rolled and burnt out; a kangaroo jumped through the hood of a sports car, causing the driver to lose control and crash; a Ford Consul rolled, righted itself, then hit a tree; dozens of other vehicles smashed radiators, axles, springs, shock absorbers, sumps, windscreens and fenders. Several cars holed their petrol tanks on hidden boulders when crossing grassy plains in the Northern Territory, Australia's most undeveloped State. Another star driver, Frank Kleinig, and his navigator, driving a Volkswagen, were knocked unconscious when they hit a wild buffalo.

Near the end-of-the-world town of Katherine, competitors encountered miles of bottomless soft sand alternating with stretches of deep red bulldust that concealed beachball-sized boulders and deep potholes. Corrugations 20 inches deep slashed the road further on. One competitor left the road when a frill-necked lizard that had climbed aboard during a tire change suddenly scuttled up the leg of his pants.

Then a new hazard appeared.

Drivers setting out at dusk on a 270-mile stretch of dirt "road" wide enough for only one vehicle were warned that a semi-trailer laden with 16 tons of high explosives was approaching from the opposite direction. No one hit it, fortunately.

Many drivers who damaged their cars on remote stretches of road used amazing ingenuity to keep them going to the next control point. The ill-fated Kleinig shattered his Volkswagen's front suspension on a rock outcrop concealed in bulldust, but improvised a front-end from a sapling and limped on to the next town. A competitor in a Vanguard he had rolled several times kept his car in the Trial with the aid of an ax and a sledge hammer—when the roof sagged down on to his head, his navigator belted it back into approximate shape with the hammer; damaged fenders that began to sag down onto the tires were hacked off with the ax! A Peugeot driver who damaged his front suspension built a log fire and with a hammer, black-smithed his wishbones, etc., back into shape. Another driver substituted mulga roots for damaged springs.

Near Port Hedland, in West Australia, largest State in the Commonwealth, the treacherous Pardoo Sands claimed many cars. A Chevrolet and a Customline sank up to their bodywork and ultimately revved their engines off their mountings trying to extricate themselves. On the Gibber Plains of mostly unsettled South Australia, Carl Kennedy, until this stage among the leaders, ruined 21 tires on one 100-mile stretch.

Gibbers are rock chips and splinters that carpet millions of acres of barren land in South and West Australia, remnants of boulders that have exploded on cold nights while contracting to normal size after expansion caused by daytime temperatures of 180° F. Only a two-inch thick "crust" flakes off with each explosion, so a large boulder takes centuries to be reduced to "gibbers." Many of them are still exploding, during the summer period, to the consternation of trans-continental visitors "camped out" in tents or caravans for the night. On an active night, conversation is impossible against the irregular, echoing cannonade.

A tiny Renault, the only vehicle in the 1955 Trial that had also completed the course in both previous Round Australia events, had its fuel pump smashed by a rock only 40 miles from a control point where a "rest and repairs" break of 24 hours was scheduled. Its driver got the vehicle to town—on the end of a freight "train" drawn by 40 mules. Three Holdens lost their bearings in South Australia and struck out into the trackless wilderness a full 90 degrees off course. For eight days they wandered aimlessly with no road or landmarks to guide them, drivers and navigators sustaining themselves on the emergency rations each car was required to carry under Trial Regulations. They stumbled onto a town 18 hours after their food and water had run out.

During the final stages of the 21-day Trial, rain turned roads into quagmires and competitors had to travel at high speeds to keep their vehicles skating, barely under control, over the slippery mud.

Any car that lost momentum on a soft spot immediately sank to the floorboards. Competitors who became stuck walked out of their shoes, which the ooze quickly swallowed, while trying to lever their vehicles out of the muck with fence posts and tree branches.

A Humber Snipe, going well over the section, shot over a rise at high speed and the crew found themselves faced with a choice of a bogged beer wagon, a deep culvert, or the bush. They chose the bush, stalled the motor, then couldn't start it again because mud had jammed the starter motor. Their only hope was the beer wagon, but it was stuck too. So they unloaded 110 barrels of beer, deditched the truck, used it to haul their Humber Snipe from the mud, reloaded the beer, all 11 tons of it, cleaned and replaced their starter and pressed on, having failed to persuade the truck driver to tap a keg for them.

The Trial had its lighter moments, of course—apart from "Gelignite" Murray's horse play with gorilla masks and toy balloons. Top Sydney driver Bill McLachlan filled his Ford Customline with mud crabs on the west coast and gave them away by the dozen to crews of stranded, broken-down vehicles he encountered while crossing the 1000-mile wide Nullarbor Plain. Mud crabs are one of Australia's top table delicacies and have been highly praised by visiting gastronomes.

There were some ugly moments during the Trial, too. Many non-trade-sponsored private entrants became incensed at various rest-and-repairs control centers when they observed teams of highly trained mechanics waiting to service company-backed vehicles.

At every control point where there was a rest period of an hour or more, 15 crack Volkswagen mechanics swarmed all over the little German cars, fitting new tires, cleaning points, plugs and carburetors, greasing the vehicles and changing oils. This highly trained team, comprised of Germans, Czechs, Englishmen and Australians, were flown around the course in specially chartered planes and were ready to give the Volkswagens assistance at any point where they could land.

On the home run to Sydney from Melbourne, capital of the State of Victoria, a distance of only 600 miles, many of the battered vehicles that had managed to cover the "first 10,000" (miles) found the tortuous and highly dangerous alpine section too tough. They dropped out like flies.

Keith Thallon, mentioned earlier, crashed badly, wrecking his car. A Holden skidded and rolled at a bad corner near Mansfield, 80 miles from Melbourne—to the delight of a group of yokels who had gathered at just that corner to watch city slickers run out of road.

Within 200 miles of the finish line, the entire remaining field of approximately 50 cars became hopelessly bogged in a muddy paddock. Several were there for eight hours. The two leading Volkswagens and several other vehicles were hauled through by 4-wheel drive trucks that had been standing by at the trouble-spot. A farmer in a heavy tractor hauled 14 more contestants out before he, too, became bogged.

The remaining drivers helped each other to manhandle their vehicles through.

Finally, the Trial ended in complete confusion, when officials penalized the apparent winners (the two Volkswagens) because examination showed their cars were "structurally damaged." Under the rules of the Trial, points are deducted for damage to chassis, axles, and other vital parts, but not for superficial dents and scratches. Other contestants were penalized because they had replaced essential parts that had been broken during the Trial. (Only tires, headlamps and windscreens could be replaced without loss of points.) Many drivers had fitted new springs, shock absorbers and similar parts.

However, a full month later, after innumerable protests and enquiries by fact-finding committees, when contestants' appeals had all been heard and officials and newspapers had calmed down, it was announced that the original apparent winners were, in fact, the ultimate winners.

First place: Volkswagen, driven by Melbourne journalist Laurie Whitehead; second place: Volkswagen, driven by Sydney professional Eddie Perkins; third place: Standard Vanguard Spacemaster, driven by Malcolm Brooks, veteran country driver from New South Wales.

All places were—to put it very mildly indeed—*well earned*.

THE PSYCHOLOGY OF MOTOR RACING

by Raymond de Becker

That motor racing is dangerous is an undeniable fact. It has killed hundreds, participants and spectators alike, and it will probably kill many more. Why, then, does anyone in his right mind court so deadly a mistress? Why do otherwise intelligent men—lawyers, doctors, psychiatrists—put on flameproof coveralls and crash hats, slide into their racing cars, and set off to do battle with others at average speeds of 100 to 140 mph? Raymond de Becker ventures an answer. Although not a competitor himself, he expresses the complex drive with insight as well as objectivity.

Motor races are just as essential a part of modern life as gladiatorial combats were in ancient Rome. One could not imagine a world without these ebullient manifestations in which it is hard to say whether the spectacle or the technical and sporting interest provides the most cogent appeal.

Leaving aside for the moment the makers and drivers, who are the real protagonists of these marathons, their attractions for mere spectators are by no means obvious. In so far as mass psychology is an unconscious psychology we must believe that they are complex, if not indeed contradictory. Long study and meticulous investigation would be needed to distinguish these attractions, and this article is but the reflection of a layman and a superficial approach to a subject that deserves to be probed far deeper.

Obviously the technical interest is not the predominant one for the mass of the spectators, although many may consider it as such in order to salve their conscience. On the other hand, the constantly growing number of motorists gives rise to a phenomenon which is only apparently a paradox, namely that the trend in motor-car construction is towards machines for which notions of mechanics are less and less useful. As Mr. Maurice Philippe pointed out in an issue of *L'année automobile,* nowadays a car must run without its owner having to know anything about its organs or do any maintenance work, which is becoming the monopoly of service stations. Naturally enough some motorists regret this trend. But it satisfies the covert laziness of the majority for whom their car is a mere convenience. If they still take an interest in the typical features of the various makes it is often aesthetic rather than technical.

To what extent does beauty constitute a mass attraction? This attraction must be very strong, for experience proves that a handsome car can achieve an enduring fame in spite of its technical shortcomings. We can all remember the Cord which owed its popularity exclusively to its pleasant shape. Furthermore, this attraction seems to meet a need of our modern world. In antiquity and the Middle Ages there was a sort of connivance between art and life which has now been lost. Beauty penetrated daily life in a way which we miss desperately today. Painting, architecture and the drama had a collective function which now no longer exists. Today, cinema stars excepted, the people we call artists live on the margin of society and their works are often without roots. Beauty—at least the kind of beauty accessible to the uninitiated—apparently only finds its way back into modern life through the machine. In a supersonic aircraft or an aerodynamic motor-car there is beauty in the pure state— a distillation of beauty the like of which is only to be found in Greek marbles. It is neither by painting, sculpture nor poetry that the spirit of ancient Greece has reentered the modern world, but through the master coachbuilders of the motor industry and the designers of aircraft. The perfection of certain cars restores beauty to everyday life. The motor-car, in a world where everybody can hope to own one, has the same place in man's life as a picture or a work of art. It is one of the most beautiful things he can buy and at the same time the closest to his real self. It is the materialization of a mechanical truth and a useful instrument as well.

In motor races, where the newest, purest and strongest models are presented in the trial stage, this beauty assumes an epic character which is one of its essential qualities and exerts an irresistible fascination on the masses. To the formal exaltation of the machine is added a human exaltation —that of the driver and the champion. It is not without cause that sporting journalists employ an epic language and, with an enthusiasm that sometimes evokes a smile, compare racing drivers to the heroes of Homer or the Knights of the Grail. When, at his last race at Le Mans, Levegh appeared in his Mercedes, crowned with his blood-red helmet, he embodied in the eyes of many the marvellous and tragic image of man and machine made one, which is the image of the world to come. They realized the truth of Rainer Maria Rilke's words: "the beautiful is but the first degree of the terrible."

Champion drivers enjoy less popularity than movie stars. Their real personality remains concealed and they have to share their glory with their machines. The public may take an interest in, or be thrilled by a Fangio, or a Moss, but this interest is not sufficient to distinguish them from the cars they drive. Beyond and above them is the rivalry between marques. It is not the man alone that conquers glory; even in the moment of victory he is one with his machine. He is stripped of his individuality and enclosed in a sort of anonymity unknown in sports where success is due to human effort alone.

We may ask ourserlves whether the masses are not drawn to motor races by a sort of unconscious quest—to discover in the bond between driver and car a revelation of modern man's relationship to the machine. Racing drivers are exceptional people no doubt, but it is precisely those who reach the limits of human capacities that give us a magnified image of what we ourselves could, or would, like to do. Thus a motor race resembles a theatrical performance in that it offers us the possibility of realizing vicariously or by anticipation a craving we feel but dare not yield to entirely.

One must not be duped by the fun-fair atmosphere typical of these great popular manifestations. Whenever the masses come within range of anything exceptional or taboo they feel the need to surround themselves with a noise and vulgarity apt to distract them from their everyday cares as well as from the real significance of the act itself. It suffices to attend a large-scale pilgrimage or great religious manifestation to know that they are always associated with a certain lusty, vulgar merriment. One has only to go to the procession at Furnes, to Lourdes, or to any Eucharistic Congress to be plunged in a jamboree quite comparable with those organized in connection with motor races. Sensitive people are shocked by what is really an instinctive defense against the rare and risky, a way of numbing one's feelings and cheating oneself. At the circus, too, one feels the need for a noisy excitement that conceals the anguish caused by the hair-raising feats of some performers and helps one to shed one's everyday mentality and suppress the inevitable doubts and anxieties.

The peculiar atmosphere essential to the spectacle depends on the apparently carefree noisy throng, the bustling officials, the reporters scurrying about for gossip or rumor, the bars where drinks to the competitors are on the house, the tub-thumping publicity, the multicolored tents in honor of the great god Oil, the seething crowd of drivers, mechanics and helpers. Just as indispensable are the vociferous loudspeakers, the bursts of popular tunes, the voice of the announcer who plays the part of the Greek chorus and expresses the feelings of the crowd, whether it is thrilled, indignant, ironical, discouraged, enthusiastic or wild with admiration. That the general excitement is merely a screen to conceal anguish or awe is clearly proved by the uncanny silence that suddenly shrouds the tense multitude at the start, when two competitors are racing neck and neck, when an accident occurs, or at the finish. They all know that every minute is fraught with danger—for the maker, the danger of seeing his hopes shattered in a fraction of a second; for the driver, the danger of accident, injury, death. Such instants of supreme concentration reveal the deep significance of these manifestations—the taste for holy horror, the thirst for a thrill, the urge to break the bonds of everyday life, to rise above the commonplace, to touch the limits of human nature, to feel the hand of death.

In motor races the hand of death feels very close. The impression is heightened by the blast of air as the cars hurtle past, the scream of tires, the roar of engines and flashes of flame from open exhausts. And though the spectators have every intention of running risks only by proxy, it happens that wilful fate panders overzealously to a taste that conscience scarcely dares admit. At Le Mans death reaped 82 victims in a matter of seconds.

In no other sport or collective manifestation is the danger of death so imminent. Some motor races, like the 500 Miles at Indianapolis, can show tragic records. Bill Vukovich, the winner in 1953 and 1954, was the 46th victim of that classic event. In comparison, track races, equestrian contests, even bicycle races which act as a magnet to huge masses of people, are harmless, peaceful pastimes. Mountain climbing and bullfighting alone possess the same deadly aura. But in the bullfight death exerts a different kind of attraction. It is bound up with the struggle between man and beast, with the grace of the ballet, and satisfies ancient dreams of the exaltation of violence and victory of man over the beasts. Mountain climbing, instead, is a sport in which death has no spectators.

In motor races death assumes a very modern aspect. It manifests itself in the midst of a crowd, accompanied by explosions, noise and flames—an irresistible vision of the fate that might befall any of us in case of war. Undoubtedly the blast, the explosion and the fire that accompany accidents in motor races are among the fundamental factors of their fascination for the unthinking masses. In "The Racers," a film made to extoll this sport, the accidents were multiplied, which illustrates the producer's view of what the public wants.

It is superfluous to insist on the competitive aspect of motor races, for they share it with other sports. It must be mentioned, nonetheless, for what it adds to their violent, even warlike, character. Moreover, this competition differs from that which we find in athletic sports. It is less individual, more collective, almost anonymous. I do not refer merely to the units or teams to which the drivers belong, but still more to the fact that the champions stand out against a background of collective rivalries, of industrial and economic struggles. Whereas an athlete owes his victory to his personal efforts alone, the aircraft pilot or motor-car driver owes his—at least partly—to the firm for which he competes. He does not exist independently but only as a member of a group. And, humanly speaking, this group is a completely different thing from a sports team. It is a largely anonymous entity of whose ins and outs the driver knows nothing and whose decisions are determined by financial resources, power politics and technical capacities on which he has no influence whatsoever.

Thus the spectators of a motor race are fed in small doses a sort of impersonal uproar, a peace-time projection of modern warfare in which the most heroic individuals are no more than finely tempered weapons wielded by the collective forces of industry and finance. In the midst of a merry holiday atmosphere these spectators can form a vague idea of what their situation would be, should historic happenings occur. This foretaste of the future remains, as a rule, below the level of consciousness, but under circumstances like those at Le Mans it can present analogies whose evidence is blindingly clear even to the most superficial observer. Here

99

we have a revelation of the ruthlessness common to war and to these great contests, and can see, on scenes of such different magnitude, the same passions producing the same effects. That the revelry continued while doctors and nurses bustled round the victims shows how much some part of man desires and enjoys this closeness to death. Dancing on the edge of a volcano has ever cast a spell over mankind which sees no value in life unless there is a risk of losing it and only discovers its meaning when life and death stand face to face and can be tasted simultaneously.

If it is true that people consider a motor race as a show and search the conduct of the actors for a revelation of what they themselves might possibly do or be, then we can no longer be satisfied with studying these manifestations from the outside, as we have done so far, but must penetrate the psychology of the spectator via that of the driver. That the latter serves the former as a model, a mirror or even a guinea-pig, appears beyond doubt when we note that the popularity of motor racing increases with the number of cars per head of the population. It is not in the countries where cars are scarce and might have the appeal of the exotic that they draw the biggest crowds. On the contrary, it is just where everyone can hope to become a motorist himself. There the racing drivers offer these beginners in mechanics the illusion of what they would like to be but do not dare, and enable them to experience vicariously and at minimum cost a relationship with the machine which is their constant preoccupation.

The importance of motor races, apart from their dangerous nature, resides in this relationship between man and machine which is one of the unsolved problems of our age.

This relationship between man and machine is no mere extrinsic phenomenon but an intrinsic reality which may be interpreted on the subjective plane. Dreams prove, in fact, that the unconscious adjusts itself perfectly to these modifications of exterior life and with baffling ease seeks its symbols in the mechanized world just as it did formerly in the animal world. Thus the horse is replaced by the car and Jupiter's eagle by the airplane. But analysis shows that these animal or mechanical objects are but the symbols of an interior reality. They express in dreams the nature of our vegetative life, instinctive or sexual. Consequently the substitution by the unconscious of car or plane for horse or eagle assumes an uncanny and disturbing significance. It means that the instinct or sexuality of modern man is no longer assimilated to a living animal but to a machine. It is not only our bodies that we mechanize by means of the engines we employ; our very instinct is becoming mechanized.

The champion motor-car driver has not the same physique as the champion athlete. He tends to become flabby; sometimes even fat. His aim is no longer to achieve a supple, powerful, balanced physique, a happy harmony of mind and muscle, but an entirely new relationship between man and a body which is foreign to him. The ancients already dreamt of a fusion of this kind and imagined the myth of the centaur. But that was a fusion of human and animal natures—a revenge, so to speak, of the animal over the human. The modern centaur sets aside his animal nature. For him it no longer exists but is replaced by a mechanism.

Like great athletes, the champion driver is something of an ascetic. But if training for Olympic sports demands physical privations and a corporeal discipline, which is often very severe, it is always aimed at a heightening of the physical faculties. The asceticism of the racing driver has an entirely different object. The physical form he requires is that most apt to make his reflexes fine and precise, his mind clear and detached, his decisions rapid and right, for they must be taken in a split second and on them his life itself depends, and in fine to give him the endurance indispensable for a nervous effort which is often long and monotonous. It is an asceticism that tends towards a sort of dematerialization and whose ultimate result might well be a muscular decline. Seated at the wheel and one with his machine, the driver is no longer a man dragged down by the mass of the earth and confined within the limits of his meagre corporeal capacities, but a new being with ten-fold powers, a god who annihilates distance and, in an aircraft, an angel who scours the heavens. The higher the speed, the further this sort of dematerialization develops, the more the sense of power—even of omniscience—grows, the more too the psychic faculties are exalted and sharpened to the point where man is transformed into a pure spirit.

The week-end driver, the family man who never pushes his car beyond 40 miles an hour, the travelling salesman torn between prudence and a thirst for speed, all feel, more or less confusedly, this emancipation from the body realized by the machine. They do not always put it in words; nor do

101

they know how far one can go in that direction. In motor races the champions pinpoint potentialities and limitations and embody, as perfectly as is possible, here and now the mysterious fusion of man and machine.

If this fusion is still a mystery it is because we do not really know whether man or machine is the preponderant partner in the connubium. Some say that nowadays cars are too fast for the drivers to control them. Others retort that it is man who goes too fast and the car cannot keep up. This contradiction is merely apparent, for the speed of the machine is a fruit of man's spirit, passions and impatience, which do not consider the limits and shortcomings of the flesh. Impatience is the cause of many accidents; it is a defiance of fate, a challenge to nature, a thirst for the impossible. We may well ask if it does not partake of the death instinct which seems to imbue, without their realizing it, the crowds that watch motor races and which we now find in the champions themselves. The latter are gamblers with danger, lovers of extremes, apprentice sorcerers, heroes who are dissatisfied with the routine of everyday life and seek compensation in what is rare and perilous.

But these men are also witnesses to the joy the machine can give. They demonstrate that between men and machine there can be a fusion which, though dangerous, can create harmony if kept within certain bounds. Man's limbs are prolonged by the organs they control and the car finally acquires a personality which brings it close to a living being. Our very language confirms this when we speak of breeds of cars as we do of breeds of horses, or call a car a thoroughbred or say it is safe or vicious, depending on whether or not it warns us that the limit of speed is near. There are affinities between certain drivers and certain cars and their mysteries are revealed to some and not to others. Those who realize this connivance with the machine are able to perceive variations of tone which are imperceptible to the common run of motorists and warn them that a defect is developing long before others would notice it. Not only does each make possess a shape and line that determine its exterior personality, but its engine has a voice that is like the expression of its soul. You can distinguish a Ferrari, a Jaguar or a Mercedes by the rhythm of their respirations.

Is this mere literature? Or may not this happy connivance between man and machine open the door to an unknown world? Might not the animal be no more than a machine brought to perfection and the machine a potential animal? Shall we perhaps discover that robots have souls or that what we call the soul of man is merely the sum of innumerable mechanical memories? Might not our dream-assimilation of horse and car go deeper than we think and lack the pejorative significance we still give it? Might not the creator still have too poor an opinion of his work and fail to see that it partakes of his own nature? Let us leave the philosophers to solve these mysteries which, however, are part and parcel of the motor races. The hundreds of thousands of people who flock to these week-end jamborees do so to ask their heroes whether they should remain mere men or place greater confidence in a mechanized world that tempts them and yet arouses their distrust.

Our knowledge of heroes would lead us to think that champion drivers are being favored or afflicted by a protracted boyhood. It has been frequently observed that speed demands a sort of miraculous youth which refuses to recognize cares and dangers, a kind of superior irresponsibility. What little we know about champion drivers shows that they keep the routine of their daily life completely separate from the turmoil in which they are involved by the race. In private life Alberto Ascari was a "quiet man" with a tame, middle-class appearance. Fangio in plain clothes is a clever, modest, reserved businessman. One is tempted to say that one part of these men has remained below their possibilities while the other is exalted to a far higher level. They have not discovered how to achieve greatness in daily life and can only do so at the wheel and at breakneck speed. In J. A. Gregoire's novel "Vingt-quatre Heures du Mans" the figure of the champion is tellingly depicted in Roger Giraud who, passive and defenseless in the presence of ordinary people and events, redeems himself only in the presence of his machine.

Do not most men feel a similar impotence when faced with everyday reality? Do they not regret their inability to raise their lives to the level of their dreams? The champion has not succeeded any better, but he at least has refused to yield and in his proudest moments makes up for the mediocrity of his day-to-day existence, realizes his dreams and surrounds himself with the gilded halo of glory. That is why all those who have resigned themselves and regret it, who

103

would like to pull themselves together and hesitate to do so, seek to rekindle their childhood's dreams by watching those who live by them.

If champion drivers draw huge crowds it is because they embody the most deeply rooted dreams of our age. A certain distaste for the earth, an urge towards freedom from the limitations of the body, a thirst for power associated with a desire for minimum effort, characterize this age which fears its conquests while extolling them. Champions embody these desires and fears and all the doubts of the world in the presence of the machine.

Their testimony proves that mankind has reached a dangerous corner, a point of cleavage where the best or worst may happen. This is confirmed by the number of fatal accidents at motor races. The champions, in their boyish innocence, bear the brunt of experiments of which the rest of us will draw the conclusions. They like playing with fire and naturally they get burnt. Boyhood's fineness, heroic daring, love of beauty, the taste for the machine, the instinct of death, meet in a reality that offers plenty of food for thought. These exceptional individuals are always placed in the most exposed positions and yet it is they who prepare and complete the great historic mutations. I believe the basic urge that draws the masses to motor races is an intuition of these mutations. Modern man seeks to perceive what fate the machine holds in store for him and to experience vicariously the pangs of death and rebirth it involves. He wants to know if he can become the superman who defies the laws of space, the mechanized centaur he visualizes in the champion, and avoid the catastrophe which alarms yet attracts him as flame does a moth.

SPEED WAS HIS SPUR

by Dennis May

In considering the qualities one finds in a man like the late Sir Malcolm Campbell, the subject of this expert profile by Dennis May, we think back to a conversation May had with another great record-breaker, John Rhodes Cobb. May asked Cobb how it felt to go 400 miles per hour—and received, in part, this answer: "Between 120 and 250 mph—the second-gear range—the sensation is like a power dive in a fighter plane. The seat back punches you in the spine. Before you have time to realize it, the jerking needles of the rev counters are closing up on the 3500 rpm deadline for the final snap into high. The shift completed, you involuntarily cram yourself an inch lower in your seat. Your throttle foot is hard against the stop. The song of 2500 horsepower rises to brain-clubbing crescendo. The banner marking the start of the miles rears over the horizon; in an instant you are up to it. In another flick of an eyelid, it has swooped overhead and gone. . . . You try focusing your eyes on a point on the guide line that is maybe a quarter-mile distant, but before the squint is halfway made the imagined speck is battering against the front of your brain, then rushing away astern. The Sierra Nevada mountains that rear abruptly out of the desert 15 miles away seem to project themselves at you with nightmarish rapidity. . . ."

What kind of men can defy Nature in such hair-raising fashion? Dennis May is here to tell us of one man who did.

The British are said to prefer their heroes "slightly unsuccessful." If this is true, it would partly explain why the late Sir Malcolm Campbell never actually progressed beyond the foothills of personal popularity.

When Sir Malcolm died in 1948, at the age of 63, he was nine times breaker of the land speed record, fastest powerboat driver in the world, and had more physical courage than a trainload of Gunga Dins. Yet, public opinion held no hint of the shocked dismay which colored the obituaries of Sir Henry Segrave, 18 years earlier. The Irish-born Segrave's farewells called him the "hero of the century," for he was Campbell's greatest rival for speed honors. But the tributes tendered Campbell in these closing hours of 1948 were statistical . . . measured . . . dry. Quite probably there was no room for elegiac flights of prose when all the necessary dates and numerals had been written down. For it is men like Campbell, with their vast list of records, who have turned the business of statistics gathering into the great swivel-chair industry it has become.

However, there is another reason why this phenomenally courageous man was more admired than loved by his countrymen. While British tradition *prefers* its heroes slightly unsuccessful, it positively *demands* from him an "eggcup ego." And Campbell's ego, to be quite blunt, was a little too healthy. It refused to narrow itself to the standard set by his attainments . . . not that Sir Malcolm cared, particularly.

It wasn't a question of conceit. For Campbell's vanity expressed itself in such harmless ways as plastering the walls of his home with photographs and drawings of himself and his speed conveyances; a procedure hardly calculated to get in anyone's tresses. And, according to the rules, it should have been necessary to twist his arm to get him to face a camera, talk into a microphone or write a book about himself. But it wasn't. He simply came forward quietly when the lenses and microphones appeared. A study of his literary output leaves little doubt that the life and the times of Malcolm Campbell were the author's best loved themes. Author of many books, motoring correspondent of the London *Daily Mail*, and editor of a well-known newsreel, he naturally had a wide journalistic acquaintance. So whenever he set off for one of the remote and heathen lands into which his unsatiable thirst for adventure led him, his fellow scribes generally got wind of it. They then sat down and began shooting off their typewriters about it.

There were enough facts in Campbell's life to exhaust the adjective potential of the wildest Hollywood publicity man. But it is the analysis of his motives that gets the student guessing.

In his "My Thirty Years of Speed," less than two of the 266 pages were given to this question of WHY? "The country responsible for the car gains in prestige," he wrote, which would indicate his desire to do all for England. But according to those closely associated with his speed attempts, this was the truth without being the whole truth. Certainly he was a patriot, and scientific advancement meant much to him. But there were two other factors in the equation.

Campbell followed Emerson's counsel: "Always do what you are afraid to do," because an irresistible inner force compelled him. The question of money never entered his attempts. While the bonuses he collected from the makers of speed products must have made a comely stack, they were dandruff alongside the sums he lavished on successive Bluebirds (which was the name given all of his record-holding cars).

Between 1924 and 1935, Sir Malcolm Campbell doubled the land speed record in nine different tries, the first being on the sands at Pendine, Wales, in September, 1924, and the speed 146.16 mph. Driving a Sunbeam car, powered by a 350 hp aero engine, he beat the record of the Italian Fiat and laid the foundation for Britain's supremacy in the field. Only once was this supremacy interrupted . . . by the late Ray Keech, an American. The last of his records on land stood at 301.13 mph, and he used a gigantic, Rolls-powered "Campbell Special," weighing five tons and delivering 2500 hp.

Newsmaking landmarks on the ladder of velocity were his specialty . . . almost an obsession . . . and thus he was first to pass the century and a half (150.86 mph, Pendine, 1925), first to beat four miles a minute (249.09 mph, Daytona, 1931), first past the two and a half centuries (253.97 mph, Daytona, 1932), first to exceed 300 mph, which is another way of saying five miles a minute (Bonneville Flats), all-time fastest on British soil (174.88 mph, Pendine, 1927), and all time fastest on sand anywhere (276.16 mph, Daytona, early 1935).

His land speed records alone were a record in themselves —nine, all told, as against three for John Cobb and three apiece for Captain George Eyston, the late J. G. Parry Thomas and Henry O'Neill Dehane Segrave.

It remains one of fate's sourest ironies that Campbell, after surviving dozens of spine-crimping escapes from death on land, sea and in the air, but mostly at the wheel of a racing car, should breathe his last in bed. No special knowledge is needed to appreciate the awful hazards involved in traveling faster than man has ever traveled before. The tire problem alone makes the outcome of every speed attempt unpredictable. The tiniest irregularity of the surface of the race course can annihilate directional stability in a split second. While elaborate testing machinery in the laboratory may attempt to reproduce high speed conditions, a huge gulf yawns between theory and practice. No robot yet made has been able to subject tire casings to the searing cross-stresses set up when a five-ton bombshell slews broadside at five miles per minute.

Campbell knew, every time he went after the land speed record, that his survival chances were around 40-60, or worse, even when conditions were ideal. When the surface was substandard, as they are apt to be on such a flighty medium as sand or salt, he went right on. If his own imagination and experience hadn't told him what the odds were, the fate of his ill-starred rivals would have. Anything could happen, and most things did happen . . . to Campbell. The more one studies his career the more one is convinced that his temperament demanded the blood-chilling succession of near misses which befell him. It was as though he knew he led a charmed life and must constantly nudge his guardian angel to make sure she was not lying down on the job.

And it was generally a tire which served as Sir Malcolm's two-way ticket to paradise, though it would be an injustice to the men who shod successive generations of Bluebirds, to suggest that the casing failure was the *primary* difficulty. Sometimes a tire would go first, causing the car to run berserk, but more often it was the berserking spasm itself, which caused the tire failure . . . generally because of the sheer inability of the rear wheels to transmit the hurricane of power to the ground. The following chronological survey of episodes tells its own story:

1924: Fanoe Island, off the Danish coast. 350 hp Sunbeam (Bluebird which later surpassed 150 mph). Both rear casings ripped off at 140 mph. Campbell fights car to standstill in lurching, screaming skid. Re-boots and tries again. This time skid comes first. Campbell hauls steering wheel into corrective lock. Front tire flips off rim like a tiddleywink, ending up hundreds of yards away.

1927: Pendine. Object: three miles a minute. Bluebird, a revised version with 630 hp Napier engine, hits water-soaked patch of sand at 170 mph. Slews into a mad waltz, cutting down a half-mile row of marking posts like a bowling ball. Slithers to a rest with one tire so badly slashed that light shows through.

1928: Daytona Beach. "The worst experience of my life." Bluebird repowered to 900 hp, strikes bump near end of measured mile at 200 mph. Begins to act like a fish-tailing Brahma rodeo bull. Flails broadside at above-mentioned speed, throwing Campbell nine inches out of the seat. Wind tears goggles away from eyes and leaves them unprotected against the sand blast from the wheels. Tires miraculously hold to rims, though no one ever knew how.

1929: Verneuk Pan, desolate baked mud lake-bed in South Africa. Failing to beat Segrave's new mile record of 231.44 mph, Campbell determines to try again, in spite of the warnings that his tires have surpassed their one-mile life expectancy. In the two required runs of opposite directions, tears every square inch of tread from all four tires. Re-tires. Lets go with 1000 hp. One tire treadless before Campbell is out of low gear. Prays. Keeps his foot down. Thunders through, breaking the five-mile record at 211 mph.

1933: Daytona. Course roughest ever. Campbell's left arm practically useless after wrenching muscles in a scuffle with self-opinionated gear shift during practice. Doctor warns against attempt. At top speed, revolution counter records equivalent speed of 328 mph. Actual timed speed 272.46 mph, which amounts to 56 mph slippage at the rear wheels. Probably an all-time record for tire endurance and one-armed navigating.

1935: Daytona. Course again wavy. Campbell strikes sand ridge at 280 mph. Car zooms 30 feet (official measurement) and comes down with a horrifying woomp which tears all tread off all tires simultaneously.

Americans played a more important part in the history of land speed attempts than the bald history reveals. It was the consistent rumors of American trespassers on this British preserve which more than once sent Campbell over the ocean during the thirties. At least Sir Malcolm *claimed* to believe these bits of gossip from overseas. Actually, and to his credit, he probably used these lukewarm trips from the U.S. to fan the excitement of the record attempts to white heat. He wanted an excuse for further adventure . . . adventure that age could not dull, nor custom stale. So if an ogre did not present itself for slaying, a windmill was erected by and for Don Quixote.

The soubriquet "Bluebird," attached to all the Campbell cars, dates back to 1911 when Maeterlinck's play of that name was bowling London over; it was first applied to a big French Darracq, which Sir Malcolm bought after it had been driven to victory in the 1909 Vanderbilt Cup Race by Victor Hemery.

Campbell knew a lot about cars from a practical standpoint, though he was definitely not an advanced automotive technician. What he did have was a gift for hiring brains which started where his left off, such as designers Amherst Villiers, Reid Railton, and Joseph Maina; mechanics supreme, like Leo Villa and Harry Leach. Between all these and Campbell, there existed a healthy respect. He, admiring and crediting publicly their importance in the accomplishments, and they, his common sense mechanical approach and ability to get the most out of what they had created. This is not to say that the boys to whom he paid a weekly wage regarded him with a dew-filtered and love-lit gaze. Far from it. There were times when a nice steady job in the Siberian Salt mines would have seemed a blessed surcease. For Campbell could be unpredictable in his lightning switches from chiselling parsimony to melting generosity. To Campbell's memory it must be credited that they stayed on. In fact, Leo Villa, possibly the first racing mechanic in the land, stuck with his employer to the end . . . 28 years in all.

Considering the vast difference in the speed of the first and last record-breaking Bluebirds, it is astonishing to learn that a number of main components from the 1924 Sunbeam raced to victory on the 1935 record holder . . . some 150 miles and 11 years later. The original brake mechanism and drums, for example, and the steering king-pins and stub axles survived the test. Villiers who had spent two and a half years building the original had done well, to understate the case, as had the score of mechanics who at one time or another worked night and day bringing the first Sunbeam to completion.

It was about this time (1925) that the speed record attemptors began to busy themselves with the science of aerodynamics. Because the wind tunnel tests showed that 60% of the frontal resistance was accounted for by the wheels alone, a redesigned Bluebird appeared after its original record had been broken by the old bug-a-bear Segrave. The car sported "spats" over both front and rear wheels, but it was Segrave's subsequent Golden Arrow which laid claim to the first squashed-toad, envelope body.

With terminal velocities mounting ever higher, the land speed records eventually came to be a fantastic acceleration and braking test. There were no straightaways longer than Bonneville and Daytona, and they weren't long enough for the remarkable speeds which were developing. The later Bluebirds, in order to double their traction on the "getaway," used four rear wheels instead of two. In order to stop, servo-assisted windjammer flaps, mounted behind the rear wheels, were manually operated in conjunction with conventional brakes.

In his day Malcolm Campbell owned and raced a bewildering array of cars: Darracq, Gregoire, Lorraine Deitrich, Peugeot, Bugatti, Delage, Schneider, Renault, Mercedes, Sunbeam, Riley and others. Even his best friends would deny that he ever approached the virtuosity of Britain's greatest road racing stars, Dick Seaman and H. O. D. Segrave, but a combination of wealth, skill and leech-like tenacity has left Campbell's name high in the annals of long distance classics. Actually, he had many wins to his credit, among them the first "200 Miles" at Brooklands and the Trophie Nationale at Boulogne, but his last attempts in circuit work betrayed his advanced years. Age seemed to mean little to him in his chosen specialty, however, for he was nearly 51 when he flashed across the Bonneville brine at five miles a minute.

At 60, Campbell still liked a good dust-up with other drivers on the highway, but it wasn't sufficient to be cleverer than he or have a faster car. To beat Sir Malcolm one had to start in front. On daily commuting journeys between his Surrey place and London, he loved to lie in ambush and waylay a certain important banker who used the same route. On one occasion this Midas so far forgot himself in the heat of battle as to belabor his long suffering chauffeur about the ears with a gold-headed cane, inflicting a severe case of cauliflower scalp.

My father, who flew with Malcolm Campbell in the Kaiser war and accompanied him on his France record attempts in 1923 and '24, once remarked that if he ever "wrote a psychological treatise, I should use dear old Malcolm as chapter I on arrested development!" Father was a staunch admirer of the recordman and his dear friend. He certainly did not mean this unkindly. But he told many stories to illustrate how after 63 years of glory, Campbell died at the age of 17. God provide more of us this ability.

Sir Malcolm's attitude toward medicine admirably gives us an insight into his perennial youth. Like the lad who voluntarily hangs by his eyebrows to raid a gull's nest and then fearfully evades a date with the dentist, the great driver ignored the advice of a medic concerning the kidney ailment which eventually ended his life. Completely in character was his 1925 quest of hidden pirate treasure in the Cocos Islands, and his magpie habit of accumulating dozens of articles, many identical, of which possibly one or two might eventually be needed; boxes of chocolates, packages of chewing gum, flash lamps, typewriter accessories, tobacco, pipes, radio tubes, and so on. His wardrobe was jammed full of expensive suits, yet he wore two or three of them at the most. Contradictory in his ways, he would drink a health or two at your expense when you met him at a bar and then suddenly remember a pressing engagement elsewhere. Once in his home, however, and under his roof, you were bowled over with his efforts to press upon you glass after glass of rare vintages.

Campbell was almost completely lacking in any outward signs of a sense of humor. One may peruse his writings and never run across the slightest hint of wit. The only thing that seemed to amuse him was the antics of the American comedy team of Laurel and Hardy. However, he honestly felt they could throw a few more pies at each other "like good chaps."

Malcolm Campbell described himself as a fatalist, but his actions, like those of virtually all dare-devils, revealed more than a sneaking regard for superstition. It may be because of this that he was finally laid to rest, clad in his zippered racing linen, while alongside him lay his Saint Christopher medallion, his favorite ebony elephant, his embroidered Bluebird.

THE SHORT, UNHAPPY LIFE OF THE MONZETTA

by Charles Beaumont

Charles Beaumont has tirelessly driven a variety of cars in many sports events on the West Coast, and, despite an incredible series of bad-luck breakdowns, has shown himself to be a fast, spirited driver. This tongue-in-cheek saga of the Monzetta Special reflects Beaumont's love and enthusiasm for the sport—and it also proves that a dedicated racer must *always* be able to laugh.   W. F. N.

In olden days when wars were fought by men selected for their prowess, would-be knights—too tall, too small, too awkward for their armor—stood upon the fringes of the battle grounds and watched and dreamed. On pirate vessels only half the crew donned handkerchiefs and swords and waded, slashing, into danger, while the other half looked on. A dozen lucky lions were picked by Nero, starved and set upon the Christians—yet consider all the other lions, mayhem running in their blood, who had to stay at home. It's true, it always has been true: a few are chosen. And throughout the corridors of Time, the cry echoes, "If they'd only let me out there, then I'd show the bastards!" It is a terrible sound.

We—knights, pirates, lions—were sitting over quarts of beer one evening, ruminating these and other thoughts. It may be that ours was the grimmest fate of all. Skilled to the point of genius, braver than Dick Tracy, filled with derring-do, we had been forced into the mould of Milquetoasts by an unkind destiny. A race weekend at Santa Barbara had just ended. As usual, we—John Tomerlin, Dave Watson, Ray Destabelle and I—had watched, timidly, from behind the snow fencing. Just like spectators. And each time a car would flash past, singing its derisive song, we would die most horribly, little by little, lap by lap. Until at last, weak from the sorrow only hobbled champions feel, we left. Before the Main Event.

And now we sat, the wives asleep, the suds luke-warm, a lachrymose quartet indeed. There seemed to be no answer. We had tried, as others had before us, to convert our family cars to combat work. Dave, a writer and photographer, had been the first. In the halcyon days (when everyone drove TCs and hated one another) he had entered his Morris Minor V8-60 in the lists. It had run well, but not wisely, ending, in the midst of its second race, in a geyser of scrap metal as spectacular as it was ruinous. Undeterred, Dave had then purchased a brand new 4CV Renault, which he essayed to run in the sedan race at Bakersfield. Alas, the car's endurance did not equal Dave's courage: while fighting it out for last place with a sick Volkswagen, a rod pierced the Renault's engine block like a Watusi spear, and a fine battle was ended. Ray, an engineer, had made similar attempts in his Austin-Healey 100, with depressingly similar results. John, an advertising man, had, in those same halcyon days, given the sport his all. Plunging himself inextricably into debt in order to bring his Porsche 1500 Super Speedster up to Stock, he had lasted for seven events, at which time the engine seized, the transmission broke, the brakes disappeared, and the creditors began to call. I, with incredible courage and dedication, had braved both penury and the imminent collapse of a happy home to pit my Porsche 1500 Normal against a legion of fleeter foes. I recall that a commentator once remarked of a performance of mine that "Beaumont is going like he had the Bank of America after him!" Which was true enough: the Bank of America *was* after me. And, despite obvious displays of championship ability, I, along with my compatriots, was at last forced to withdraw from the Hunt. Tearing the proud plaques from our dashes, taming the wild and hungry hearts of our cars, hiding our battle dress away in dark closets, we faced reality. We faced facts. We faced bankruptcy.

Months passed, and we all tried, very hard, to make the transition from Hero Drivers to Disinterested Spectators. We argued that there were plenty of other, less financially catastrophic hobbies to pursue. Like philately, or grunion hunting, or floral arrangements. What was the use of racing, anyway? What did it prove? So you go fast in a car, does that cut any ice immortality-wise? Childish nonsense, that was what it was. Morbid pandering to a neurotic death-wish. Who cared? Who gave a damn?

We did. Only too keenly aware of the truth of Mr. Kimberly's axiom ("If you can't afford to race, you shouldn't race") we found, nonetheless, that our spirits were falling at a rate commensurate with the rise of our economic statuses. Our expressions became hang-dog. We tended to mope about the pits at the various courses, filling our nostrils with Castrol fumes, listening like hi-fi addicts to the percussive symphony of Ferraris at peak revs, and snarling at spectators that we, too, were fast *pilotos* once and would be again, some day. Our evenings were devoted either to building model race cars or playing "Grand Prix." If anything, we were more involved with the sport than before. But it was all sham. We derived no more real satisfaction from these ersatz activities than a confirmed alcoholic who has been forced to turn to Pepsi-Cola for surcease.

The Santa Barbara event had thrown us, finally, into a state of depression so profound that a thoughtless word would have set us all to weeping like children.

"That lousy Jimmy—," said John, referring to the winner of the Under 1500 cc Production race. "I spun him out at Palm Springs. I almost lapped him at Torrey. Didn't I?"

"Truly," said Dave, "you did."

"Yeah," John said, dabbing a tear away.

"I had a watch on the leading Healey," said Ray. "Six seconds slower than I turned in '55."

"Yeah."

"If they'd only let us out there—"

"Yeah."

We sat in silence another hour. Then one of us (I shan't cause needless embarrassment by naming him) crashed his hand down on the table, made a strangled cry that sounded like "Eureka!" and began to roll about the floor, singing "Happy Days Are Here Again." We thought, of course, that the poor wretch had cracked under the pressure, but before we could make a move to restrain him, he said: "Gentlemen! I have the answer!"

"To what?" we inquired, suspiciously.

"To our problem," he said. "How idiotically simple! How stupid of us not to have thought of it before!"

"Easy, old boy."

"Yes," he responded, "*easy*. My friends, is it or is it not a fact that in this room may be found four of the fastest, smoothest, most fearsome drivers in the world?"

"A fact," we chorused, sadly.

"And is it not also a fact that, owing to a thankless, shortsighted government which will not subsidize its future champions, we have been lately denied our calling?"

"True, so true."

"Very well. Now we have found that it is not entirely feasible to race our own cars; and of course we are all too proud and sportsmanlike to accept the largesse of some wealthy entrepreneur—"

"Well," interrupted Ray, "I wouldn't go that far."

"Be still. The point I am attempting to make is this: Our worries are over. Now listen carefully." He lowered his voice to a conspiratorial whisper. "Instead of hanging separately, let us hang together. Let us pool our meagre resources and *build a Special*."

And so, with those fateful words, the die was cast. It is true that, however talented and successful we may have been in our individual professions, we were mechanical simpletons to the man; but that seemed a detail. Dave and Ray knew the principle of the internal combustion engine, John had actually assisted in the removal of a Porsche motor, once, and I . . . Well, I possessed the sensitivity that would give us aesthetic as well as technical perfection. Instantly, the following morning, we met again and put the dream on paper. After a cursory tabulation of our funds, we decided that a Class H Special would be the best bet. Something simple, economical, easy to repair, inhumanly fast and at least as handsome as a Ferrari would do.

Important things coming first, we designed a crest forthwith—a rampant turtle on a field of yellow—established and named our racing team (Equipe Tortoise), and decided upon the color of our coveralls. Then we discussed the order in which we would drive. Then we constructed a striking pitboard in the shape of a turtle.

Then, these items out of the way, we began looking for a car.

Class H automatically brought Crosley to mind, but upon making a close scrutiny of the winning machines of this marque, however mutated, we found that they were either as expensive as a Pegaso Berlinette or as complicated as an ICBM. Therefore, feeling that the Special should be practical above all else, we rejected Crosley and, after entertaining lovely dreams of Oscas, Stanguellinis, Morettis, Giaurs, etc., settled upon Panhard as our base. Did not Jean Pierre Kunstle go like Jack-the-Bear in such a Special? Had not Perry Peron and numerous others caught glory by the short hairs thus equipped?

The problem of a suitable body arose and was promptly

slapped down when, taking a constitutional one day, Dave saw what turned out to be the very first new-style Devin shell. Struck insensible by the beauty of it, he crawled, choking, to my house and presently the quartet was gathered. We knew, at once, our immediate destiny. Rough and transparent, the shell nonetheless possessed a personality that transcended anything seen in class H to date. It was sleek, fierce, graceful, and the spitting image of a Monza Ferrari. When we visualized it in bright red paint, we began to breathe heavily; when we discovered that the price was under $300, we swooned. It was beyond our wildest imaginings. A Special, we had been led to believe, must of necessity be hideous. Yet here was a body quite the equal of the finest.

Some investigation revealed that the car could be purchased in one of two forms: complete and incomplete. That is, we could place an order with Mr. Devin, close our eyes, open them, and find a race car built to our specifications; or, for slightly less, we could build the thing ourselves. As our ignorance was matched only by our enthusiasm, we naturally chose the latter.

"That way," we reasoned, "it'll be *our* car. When it nips across the line for the checkered flag, by George, we'll know *we* were responsible!"

Estimating a total cash outlay of $2,000, and six weeks of actual labor, we scampered out to Devin's factory and returned with several hundred pounds of metal parts. These we dumped in a garage we'd rented, next to Bill Corey's workshop, and went back for the body-shell which, in our haste, we'd forgotten. Envious stares accompanied our passage. Little boys dropped their yo-yos. Already we began to feel a sense of pride and adventure.

Unfortunately, the feeling was transitory. After drinking a toast to the success of the Equipe Tortoise, we found ourselves faced with the problem of transforming all of this debris into a racing car. And it did not seem quite so niggling a problem as it had before. In fact, for a moment, staring in silence at the mysterious mountain of dark metal, it seemed a large problem indeed. But, of course, none of us would admit to the slightest misgiving. We drank several more cans of beer, picked up parts, peered at them, put them down, picked up others, and called it a day.

Next morning we went at the job in earnest. A discussion of race strategy lasted until noon, then we had a leisurely lunch and, around 3:00, rolled up our sleeves. The first discovery was not joyous. Either the frame did not fit the body or the body did not fit the frame. Ray was the first to laugh it off, explaining, out of his years of engineering experience, that obviously we would have to lengthen the body or shorten the frame. It seemed logical. So we took the frame and had it shortened five inches and narrowed four. That it came very close to fitting filled us with enormous satisfaction. Dave, by dint of his photographic experience, was elected head welder, and within no more than three months, we had most of the brackets, mounts, and other attaching parts fastened. What was lacking in professional polish was more than compensated for in bulk. Each weld was the size of a clenched fist, and this gave us great confidence.

An automotive writer named OCee Ritch dropped by at that point in the proceedings and, finding himself bemused by our operation, helpfully described what we were doing. For the technically minded, I shall quote him, briefly:

"The completed frame weighs less than 75 lbs., is sufficiently rigid to sustain the independent suspension favored by Panhard and accepts the stock rear end. The rear axle torsion bar unit from the Panhard roadster bolts right on. . . . The front end is a different story. A Fiat-style upper and lower transverse spring set-up provides independent front suspension. Sliding collar half-axles, with three U-joints per side, connect the transmission-differential combo to the wheels . . ."

All of which is doubtless true. At any rate, it was necessary for Dave to quit his job and work six to twelve hours every day to accomplish the above, and on the fourth month it must be admitted that tenacity had replaced enthusiasm. Between the golden hills of empty beer cans and the black hills of engine parts, we moved like damned souls doomed to work at a jig-saw puzzle for eternity.

One of the greatest disappointments came when we discovered that the engine compartment would not, could not accommodate the engine. It rose hideously four inches above the hood or bonnet line, and not all of our piety nor wit could erase an inch of it. The best answer, of course, was to have foreseen the difficulty in the first place. Now, to retain the smooth Ferrari line, we would have to tear everything down again and, to all intents and purposes, start from scratch. Which, of course, was unthinkable. Yet ruining the effect of our car by allowing great metal chunks to extrude was equally unthinkable. For one thing, everyone would know

118

it wasn't a Ferrari. And we freely admitted—*I* did, anyway—that part of the fun would obtain from deceiving uninitiated spectators into the notion that we were racing a Ferrari.

There was, alas, nothing to be done, except junk the whole project—which we considered. So, abandoning our dream in favor of a lesser one, we tearfully cut the proper holes and told ourselves that it gave the machine a savage look.

Recompensing for this disaster by installing a first class racing steering wheel and two magnificently upholstered seats, we worked blindly for another three months. By now we were feeling like veteran mechanics, it goes without saying: modifying the cam, installing a special oil cooler, re-mounting the generator, etc. At last it began to look like a car. Not the beauty we'd imagined, perhaps, but, as John commented: "If it isn't going to be pretty, by Heaven it's going to be fast!" But, truth to tell, we weren't too sure of that, either.

Still, on we labored. And as the mountain of beer cans grew, the mountain of parts diminished; until, to our collective astonishment, we found one day that we had finished.

Dave, for his above-and-beyond-the-call endeavors, was given the privilege of starting the engine for the first time. A spectral silence fell upon us. Like soldiers who had fought a long and desperate war and found themselves unprepared for Armistice, we blinked foolishly at one another. Dave slid into the cockpit. He depressed the accelerator pedal. He reached out a trembling hand.

A cough. A grinding. A wheezing. Then:

It started! We shook our heads in disbelief. *It actually started!*

That was to be one of the last unalloyed moments of joy we ever felt regarding the car, though of course we didn't know it. We did insane dances, listened to the ear-shattering pierce of the exhaust, and forgot the months of labor.

First test was to be held on the old Hansen Dam course. It had been locked against the public, but we were shrewd customers. Lifting the chain and driving beneath it was the work of a moment. A couple of hours sufficed to set the carburetors. Then Dave took off for the first lap, experiencing a certain difficulty with the horizontal-H-pattern Panhard gear-change. John and Ray and I stood there, in the sun, watching the car flick around turn one and out of sight, and we were humble and silent.

So, as it happened, was the car, shortly thereafter. One lap had rendered first and second gears unusable, and the timing was off. Unconvinced, I took it for a spin, tried to shift into second, and returned with the gear-shift in my hands. It had broken loose completely. We couldn't do much else that day, so we left, basically pleased.

The following week saw modifications to the gear-box, switching it to the normal vertical-H pattern, and an unsuccessful search for a more substantial cover-plate. The one I'd cracked was of pot-metal, but Panhard apparently had not anticipated such displays of animal strength, for pot-metal was standard for the part. We tacked on some rubber and told ourselves to be gentle.

More experiences at Hansen Dam, correcting timing, getting the carburetors set, etc. Once we managed to complete an entire lap.

Then . . . our first race; at Santa Barbara! The gear-shift was still showing a rather distressing tendency to pop out of third—still the only workable gear—and we could not seem to get the beast to fire on both cylinders; but these were trifles. Had we not lapped Hansen as fast as the third place under-1500 cc car in that venue's inaugural event? (No, we had not.) However, nothing daunted, we mailed in our entry and further alienated our wives by discussing race strategy until the small hours.

It was decided that Dave would drive on Saturday, in the qualifying event. Then on Sunday I would take it for half-distance and turn over either to John or Ray, who would flip a coin. We would not push it at all. We would simply cruise about, get to learn the undoubtedly peculiar handling characteristics of the front-drive Panhard, and otherwise go about things intelligently. Certainly we would not try to win a trophy, or (horrors!) *beat* anyone.

It is difficult to record with any real accuracy the glee we felt at technical inspection. Despite the junk sticking lewdly out of the hood, several people did inquire if it was a Ferrari. Crowds gathered. Conversation buzzed. Crosley drivers feigned disinterest. It was swell, even though we couldn't manage to fire up the engine.

Equally swell was Saturday at the course, before practice. We were neat as British waiters in our uniforms, and our car —which we had decided to call a "Monzetta"—was attracting a most gratifying amount of attention. Also, as things turned out, it was very nearly as loud as the 4.9 Ferraris and 3.0 Maseratis.

We watched the production cars line up for practice and fought our sudden terror by polishing the Monzetta's hood. Finally it was time, and Dave—the look of eagles in his eyes—hopped in. We pushed him to the grid. He started. He came around once. He came around twice. Then he did not come around.

The car had stopped running. We got it back to the pit and fiddled with it and got it working in time for the race. Again Dave took off. Two laps later he drifted in, silently, and we examined the situation and found nothing more serious than a blown engine. Specifically, a piston had disintegrated, covering the interior with a fine metallic dust.

Ray replaced the bonnet, slowly, as one would close a coffin lid, and said: "Well, we've got to get the bugs out, you know."

Many weeks and several hundred dollars later, we entered a race at Paramount Ranch. Paramount Ranch was described as a "fun course" and it certainly was that, provided your notion of fun is going at incredible speed between rows of trees, under bridges, and around chasms, with one tiny slip consigning you without adieu to eternity. Happily, it was John's turn to start things off. Beginning from dead last position, he had managed to pick off three cars when, on lap three, swooping under the bridge, the gear lever came off in his hand and he found himself hurtling toward a hill.

The Monzetta climbed the hill admirably, and rested from its promontory for the remainder of the race. Next day, *my* chance for glory was slightly diminished by a heavy rain and the loss of all gears save third, which had to be held in firmly. (We'd wired the plate back into position, welding being impossible.) One of the cylinders ceased firing after three rather fantastic one-handed laps and we retired, shaken, to the Coke stand.

"Got to get the bugs out," Dave said.

Next race was at Pomona. We had taken the transmission apart and worked over every minuscule portion of it and were sure, now, that all would be well.

Ray had starting honors this time, and our luck appeared to be on the upswing for he completed practice and Saturday's race, placing fourth in class. (He claims also to have frightened Shelby into a dramatic spin into a tree at turn six, but I can't quite see how that could have been, as the Monzetta was half a lap behind at the time.) On Sunday, however, the engine blew again. Sky-high.

121

It goes without saying, I trust, that the original budget had been somewhat overshot by now. It had, in fact, been doubled. But we were not defeated. Giving the next couple of races a miss, in order to become re-acquainted with our wives, we entered again at Pomona.

It was the scene of the Monzetta's sole achievement. Having crashed into a hay-bale during practice, Dave did not think that the car ought to be allowed to run; but we patched and pounded and persuaded, and he changed his mind. Starting from a poor position in the field, he amazed all of us—principally himself—by surging past most of our competitors on the first lap (accidentally shunting Pete Woods' inoffensive and pretty little Seidlitz Citroen 2CV Special in the process) and dogging the leader—Perry Peron—until the last lap, at which time he found an opening and went on to win the race. Our hosannas of joy were still echoing on Sunday when a perhaps over-jubilant Dave attempted to bluff a Lotus out of a turn. His lack of success was signal and he went into the hay like an ardent lover. Very little was left of the right side of the Monzetta, and, of course, the engine had decided to join the fun by ceasing forthwith to function.

At Palm Springs, I clung gamely to last place, finally ceding it because of further interior malaises. Which was as well, for, on the back straight, where it was possible to nudge 92 mph, rather frightening quantities of oil were being pumped into my face.

At Santa Barbara, ironically, the union—as well as the engine—dissolved. Getting off to a splendid start, on account of the curious firing of both cylinders simultaneously, Ray limped in after three laps; and we knew, without having to ask, what was wrong.

"Got to get the bugs—" John began, but it was no use. We'd never get the bugs out, never, and even if we did, new ones would come to take their place. Our eyes were not entirely dry that day, standing by the crippled little Special, which had, after all, done its best. It hadn't died, really. A group of idiots had murdered it. And it was with no great pleasure that we finally admitted our crime. There was a feeling of relief, perhaps, but mostly sadness. It could have been so fine; and it *was* basically a good idea. But . . .

Ray bought the Monzetta from us, but we never see the car. "It's being prepared," he tells us, and we nod and watch all the fine Devin Specials that followed our pioneering venture, all of them running well and fighting for the lead. And it makes us melancholy, but we take a certain small comfort in the knowledge that *someone* had to be first, *someone* had to blaze the trail so that others might travel safely.

And, who knows? Perhaps Ray will get it running right, eventually, and take it out, and we'll see it doing the job it was built to do. Stranger things have happened.

ASCARI'S LAST CURVE

by John Fitch

A variation on that old phrase "It takes one to know one" can legitimately be applied here, with regard to John Cooper Fitch—dean of American sports car racing. John is particularly well-qualified to write of the late Alberto Ascari. As the only American ever selected to compete on the famed Mercedes team in Europe, Fitch was able to draw upon his own specialized knowledge of speed and danger to write this stirring account of Italy's famous son. This piece originally saw print in the non-automotive pages of **The Atlantic Monthly**, reflecting the freshness and quality Fitch brings to his subject.

Alberto Ascari, like his father, died at the wheel of a racing car. Both were 36 years old and both died on the 26th of the month—twice the 13 that Alberto feared. It was a fate that his race-wise friends could have predicted for him, but who can say that the Ascaris, father and son, chose the wrong career?

The shadow of Ascari's father and his mother's fear that Alberto would follow him made Alberto aware of the stakes involved. But young Ascari was compelled to race, and at 17 he overcame his mother's opposition by threats to run away from home. Secretly at first, he raced motorcycles with moderate success until his opportunity to graduate to four wheels came in 1940 when he drove an early Ferrari in the Mille Miglia. Ascari never seemed to doubt where he was going.

His real success began with Maserati cars after the war, and at Modena in September of 1947 he had his first taste of the victory that was so sweet to him. His star rose quickly and in 1949 he was champion of Italy. From then on, he was always a driver to be reckoned with in the battle for the world's championship, and this he won with Ferrari in 1952 and 1953. He went everywhere that races were held. In Spain, South America, Italy, England, France, and Germany, his skill was polished to a razor's edge by experience and the counsel of his veteran teacher and friend, Gigi Villoresi. This was one of the closest and most successful master-protégé combinations in sports history. Villoresi was at the peak of his powers just after the war when Ascari was finding himself. Gigi, a gentle and cultivated bachelor, guided Ascari's apprenticeship and taught him his technique of cornering, which may account for a long absence of serious crashes. The secret is to brake early and drive smoothly around the corner with full power on. This gives a margin of safety as well as being fast. When the corner is entered too fast a lot of correction is necessary before the car is steady enough to take full throttle again. But Villoresi taught Ascari to concentrate on leaving the corner fast, benefiting by a higher speed all the way to the next corner.

This and a knowledge of *which* corners to leave fast and which should be entered fast in order to get the best lap speed were the key to Ascari's mastery, I think. For Alberto, these were the tips that counted; they were the inside story on the only world that mattered to a man whose star was a checkered flag at the end of a hot and dusty road.

Ascari became a hard-minded, analytical, grimly determined racing machine. However much he suffered off duty with ulcers, sleeplessness, and apprehension, behind the wheel he became a cold computer of distance, time and tires, corners and competition, and he got his checkered flags, luck and family history notwithstanding. He became stonily indifferent to danger, and the thought of such emergencies as lost wheels or broken suspensions, two of the completely uncontrollable hazards he faced, left him unmoved.

He brought a Ferrari to Indianapolis in 1952 and won the respect of everyone from the perennial railbirds to the speedway's president, Wilbur Shaw, by his masterful handling of a basically unsuitable car. The Ferraris were designed for road racing rather than for the relatively constant speeds and the greater distance of the Indianapolis event.

There were three similar Ferraris at Indianapolis that year, but their American drivers bowed to the seemingly inevitable when the cars refused to qualify. The drivers switched to the native Offenhausers. Not Alberto. Fired by pride in his Italian car, Ascari, a foreign underdog a long way from home, modified the car, changed tactics, and tried harder. Finally, with his face a picture of determination that truly approached ferocity, he forced the car to a qualifying speed, ensuring his entry in the race.

He knew where he was going all right, and he was well on his way when a collapsing wheel spun him helplessly into the infield and out of the race. He was in the northeast curve traveling at about 120 mph, not a remarkable speed until you consider the curves at Indianapolis. No one of these curves is like any other, and all are bounded on the outside by a cement wall that has proved to be immovable. The curves are slightly banked to a degree designed to prevent centrifugal loading at 85 mph, and they are all bumpy. At 120 mph, Ascari was precariously holding his heavy Ferrari to the smooth line that would carry him onto the next straightaway, while it bounced, jerking and skidding, toward the wall. At this moment the outside rear wheel, the one doing the most to resist centrifugal force, collapsed, crashing the lurching car onto the pavement in a shower of sparks. The sensation must have been something like falling through a trap door on a roller coaster. Alberto was no longer a driver, but a passenger in his spinning car as it described a large arc, at first toward the dreaded wall and then looping down into the unpaved infield where it came to rest in a cascade of plowed earth. To have a wheel collapse at a speed of more than 100 mph is not a trifling matter. But Alberto was concerned only with his next race. It was not his first or his last wheel failure. The next was in Germany.

In 1950, 1951, and 1952, Ascari had won the Grand Prix of Germany on the Nurburgring, which is known as a driver's course. Here the road twists and plunges erratically through the Eifel Mountains in a particularly wicked way that awards courage and skill a clear dividend of speed. There are few straights allowing a moment's respite and these are punctuated with humpbacked bridges which send a fast car soaring. Here, in 1951, Ascari demonstrated the high order of racecraft he commanded when, with a small lead over his old rival Fangio, he calmly drew into the pits before his last lap. The Ferrari team was frantic. Ascari wanted the tires changed before committing himself to that long (14-mile) last lap rather than risk a failure. He knew he had time to change before Fangio passed and that he could hold Fangio if he had new tires. He was right, but the strain on the Ferrari team was almost unbearable.

In 1953, his efforts to make it four wins in a row were surely the ultimate in cold-blooded determination. He had a 50-second lead over Fangio (again) one kilometer from the pits when he lost a front wheel in the fastest part of the circuit at about 140 mph. By means known only to Alberto, he not only avoided a crash but arrived at the pits at the same time as Fangio. He had covered the kilometer on three wheels only 50 seconds slower than Fangio on four wheels! Then, when most drivers would have put the brakes on and ruined the brake drum, he let the car coast to a stop even though it was beyond his pit. Furthermore, he left the engine going, so that when the mechanics arrived with a jack, he was able to drive backwards to the pit while a mechanic steered with the jack handle. With a new wheel he sailed off and his next flying lap was a record, in spite of the fact that the brake drum was damaged and out of balance. He then took over Villoresi's car, which Gigi was always glad to give to his erstwhile pupil, and set up another lap record. Just when it appeared conceivable that he could do it again and win in spite of everything, the car broke and he retired. He quietly packed his helmet and goggles into his bag, put on his customary sports jacket, and walked out of the pits to a spontaneous ovation for a man who had tried and lost.

But Ascari usually won. On that hard championship trail that kept him packing, traveling, practicing, and racing nearly every weekend, the novelty became the race Ascari didn't win. The results were almost monotonous; still no one denied full credit to his determined skill and applied racecraft. He was the idol of the *tifosi*, Italy's racing fans, and his nickname, "Ciccio" (roughly, Chubby), was universally known in Italy. The name Ciccio was a measure of his real popularity. Instead of being awed by their World Champion driver—and this is an awesome thing in Italy—his fans named him familiarly and affectionately.

Ascari was an undemonstrative, almost non-Latin, Italian whose quiet behavior was as unpretentious as his stodgy figure. A show of temperament or grandstanding of any kind was simply never suggested by anything in his public or private behavior. He didn't care for crowds or attention from the press, but he put in a dutiful appearance at the many prize-giving functions whose success depended upon his presence. After the function was over he would take a solitary walk, clearing his mind in the fresh air and looking, in his neat blue suit, a little like a respectable headwaiter after hours. He was never exuberant, but his smile came most frequently in the company of racing friends, when concerned with the familiar questions of his profession.

At Indianapolis, he whimsically solved the language problem by learning one innocuous word and using it for all occasions. Everything was "fine, fine" for Alberto at the brickyard. No one could remember such an agreeable fellow.

He was superstitious, as are most drivers whose continued well-being is dependent upon such vagaries as the flight trajectory of birds (which can knock a man out at high speed), the ability of a battered tire to resist blowout, or the good fortune to miss an invisible patch of oil dropped by another car. Good drivers often see their comrades crash for reasons which are never completely understood. The results of chance happenings on the race course are drastic enough to tempt the most literal-minded to consult astrologists. Like many another driver seeking a neutrality pact with fate, Ascari shunned black cats, the number 13, and so forth, but he also had a private anathema: the Montlhery circuit outside Paris, the road where his father died. It was too deeply fraught with association, even for Ascari.

And so Alberto Ascari became the Italian driver of his age in a country that knows racing and breeds good drivers. He was the World's Champion for two consecutive years, 1952 and 1953. Instead of easing up when on top, he demanded more of himself, became determined and dedicated to victory. His escapes became more frequent and miraculous. There never was a suggestion of retirement. He was an idol, and idols seldom quit at the peak of their powers.

It is conceivable that Ascari drove as though he could afford to die; that the circumstances of his life and times as Italy's champion demanded it of him, and that he acceded. To see him drive was to consider this possibility; for, though beautifully controlled and never wild, he used the full capacity of his car and every inch of road, leaving absolutely no margin for error.

Pressing for every second at high speed in Mexico, he anticipated a right curve over a hill but found a sharper left instead. His big Ferrari rocketed up the wall of a cut, rolled and skidded hundreds of yards down the road on its fragile alloy roof. Luckily for Ascari, the Ferrari was a coupe.

Ascari never liked the Mille Miglia or its Mexican counterpart, the Pan-American, because these long-distance, city-to-city races on the open road, which can at best be only partially remembered, did not suit his thrusting style of driving close to the border of control. His technique was better suited to the short and fierce Grand Prix on known circuits. A Mille Miglia crash in 1951 resulted in the death of a spectator, and the ensuing process of law deprived Ascari of third-party insurance until the case was settled. He therefore abstained from entering the event out of consideration for spectators until 1954, when, the case settled, he won for Lancia in one of his most glorious victories. Though he had entered with distaste and even with misgiving in a Lancia that was as yet unproved for long-distance races, he and Villoresi practiced assiduously. A truck rammed him the morning before the start, on the streets of Brescia as he set out for a final check of the first miles; but despite the unpropitious sign, he made the start and fought for 1000 miles in appalling weather to win the race least suited to his nature. He said he was especially glad for Villoresi's sake as his old friend had crashed in practice and was unable to start.

He fought a prodigious, race-long battle with Fangio and Farina at Monza in 1953 only to have his first place snatched from him on the last curve of the last lap by a crash. Villoresi crossed the line himself and rushed back, his face a mask of anxiety, to find his friend regretting only the lost victory.

In May, 1955, four days before he died, at the moment of gaining the lead in the Grand Prix of Europe, he crashed through a barrier and plunged into the harbor at Monte Carlo. He had just burst out of the dark tunnel under the Casino and rushed down the ramp to the chicane, a barricaded jog that carried the race onto the quay bordering the basin with its white yachts decked with fluttering pennants, when a snatching brake or perhaps a film of oil left by the last Mercedes, retiring at this moment in a swirl of blue smoke, upset the delicate 100 mph balance. Ascari's Lancia could not be saved. With an explosion of fence splinters and sandbags he catapulted into the harbor in a geyser of spray and steam that towered like a depth charge. For a dreadful 20 seconds the milling green surface gave up only a few oily bubbles while divers, prepared for just this emergency, scrambled into action. A pack of cars roared by, the last slowing as its driver twisted in his seat looking back. A light blue helmet bobbed to the surface, and Ascari's streaked face was beneath it. On leaving the quay he had missed a steel mooring by inches, and not to have been knocked unconscious or caught in the sinking car was a bonus of luck, but to Alberto it was "nothing, nothing."

From the brief convalescence at his home in Milan it was

only a few minutes' drive to Monza, Italy's premier circuit, where he had seen his father win in 1924. There, on the familiar road, while trying a Ferrari before the next Sunday's race, Alberto Ascari took his last curve. The curve where he crashed could be taken at full speed easily in the carefully prepared car he was driving; the exact circumstances of his death probably never will be known. The sports car he was driving was 20 mph slower than a first-class Grand Prix car at this point, which means that the Ascari talent could not have been brought to bear, much less ruffled, by the driving situation in which he died. Some say he had not recovered from the Monte Carlo crash and suffered a sudden relapse or missed a gear. Whatever happened, the racing world lost one of its finest figures of all time.

His funeral brought a day of mourning for a nation stunned with grief. Milan, the business and financial center of Italy, was as quiet as a village when the 15 canopied carriages required to carry the many wreaths inched past the silent mourners. On the black coffin rested Ascari's familiar light blue helmet. The procession was drawn by horses, feather-plumed and all black, and only the sorrowful clopping of hoofs could be heard from the streets lined with black drapes. A million people paid the only tribute left to give to a favorite prince who was lost in his full strength.

SPEED AT DAYTONA BEACH

by Peter Lyon

There are certain "small worlds" into which one can disappear without a trace, for a time at least. The world of a motion-picture crew on location, the world of a college football game, the world of a chess tournament. . . Certainly the world of motorized battle at an event such as Daytona's Speed Week would qualify in this category. Here the racing enthusiast is happily absorbed into a swirl of rev counters, checkered flags, exhaust noise—and the specialized language of wheeled competition. Peter Lyon attended one of these events at Daytona for **Holiday** magazine—and offers his own astute impressions of this colorful, gaudy phenomenon.

As a Florida resort, Daytona Beach boasts one incomparable asset—a wide, handsome strip of white, hard-packed sand 23 miles long, and all of it public, all of it free. Predictably, man has bordered this sea-begotten wonder with hot-dog stands, carnival areas, and outrageous motels which make architects shudder. No matter: nothing can rob this splendid beach of its power to bewitch. Every summer it is thronged, for Daytona Beach has no serious competition in Florida as a summer resort.

Indeed, 50 years ago Daytona Beach and its neighbor, Ormond Beach, drew most of the holiday trade even in winter. On the mainland you can still come upon the big two- and three-story frame houses built in those days; save for their girdles of azaleas and, in season, poinsettias, these houses would be seemly along the main street of any New England town. But today it is a different matter.

Today the winter tourist is likely to leapfrog over Daytona Beach, his eye fixed on the more stylish resorts to the south. Miami Beach is gaudier; Palm Beach is posher; St. Petersburg has its old folks; the Keys are closer to nature. Forgotten by fashion, Daytona Beach has few night clubs, no big-name bands, no stars of stage, screen and television;

no swank or pretension; and, what is a mortal wound to winter business, no horse races. Somewhat grumpily, Daytona Beach has been obliged to forswear glitter and to settle, in its middle age, for being what is called a family resort.

A dowdy fate, and a few civic-minded folk were disposed to fight it. Some years ago, in consequence, they organized what they called Speed Week. The thing has grown and grown until now, as such matters are measured in Florida, it even has a tiny tradition. Moreover, Speed Week has become a powerful magnet for winter tourists.

The charm of Daytona Beach in Speed Week—always scheduled for mid-February—comes from the simple, unaffected emotion that pervades the occasion. The emotion is love. Wherever you turn, you are likely to trip over citizens who are here from all over the country to celebrate their own true love, the latest model of stock car, F.O.B. Detroit.

Plenty of other species of the genus Automobile are on view around Daytona Beach during Speed Week. Glossy antiques move sedately past, hot-rods snort in the streets, European sports cars dart in and out of traffic, there are midget racing cars and even Indianapolis racing cars aplenty; and each of these, of course, is a distraction. But only briefly. Just as a man strolling with his wife will stare speculatively at a passing lovely and then, recollecting himself, affectionately press his wife's arm, so during Speed Week the automotive man, forsaking all others, renders homage to his familiar favorite.

By the hundreds he annually descends upon Daytona Beach to submit his love to various trials, to test her safety, her economy, her acceleration—and most of all her speed. Day after day during Speed Week you can find him at dawn out on the long hard smooth white sweep of beach, his grease-blackened hands proudly patting his darling's polished flanks.

He has for her inarticulate terms of endearment. She is "quite a wagon," or "a smooth job," or "one hell of a bucket," or "a sweet rig." If he seems, at this improbable hour, to be lost in concentration, likely it is because he is about to try for membership in the Century Club by driving his car over a measured mile at better than 100 miles an hour. Overhead, a dozen disdainful pelicans flap by in single file, intent on breakfast; and the tide creeps in.

As Speed Week draws to its climax, a vast press of automotive buffs assembles, drawn by the lure of the 500-mile sweepstakes for sedans and convertibles, 200 laps around the new two-and-a-half-mile Daytona International Speedway, which has been called the finest, fastest automobile race track in the world. Overnight the area's population—some 78,000—is nearly doubled. Since the whole county has only 40,000 rooms for tourists, plenty of visitors are obliged to settle for informality. They sleep in cold discomfort on the beach; they sleep in cars parked for miles, bumper to bumper, alongside the main highways leading into Daytona—any wretchedness rather than miss Sunday's big race. Here is a queer but impressive tribute to the product of Detroit's assembly lines. If ever one city had reason to admire another, the one is Detroit and the other is Daytona.

This civic infatuation was, indeed, love at first sight. As long ago as 1902 a pair of automotive pioneers, Ransom Olds and Alexander Winton, were on winter holiday at the Ormond Hotel and they fell to talking of their cars. Naturally their talk was boastful; naturally there was only one way to settle the issue: by racing their cars on the beach. So it began; and in the years that followed William K. Vanderbilt pushed a Mercedes to 92 mph; Louis Chevrolet and Henry Ford came down to Daytona with their cars; and in 1907 Fred Marriott drove a Stanley Steamer at nearly 200 mph—but he hit a bump on the beach, caught an updraft, took off, and crashed. Barney Oldfield and Ralph DePalma coursed down these same sands; and later, in 1929, there was Sir Henry Segrave in his Napier-Sunbeam, roaring along at 231.362 mph; and then, in 1935, Sir Malcolm Campbell in his *Bluebird* at 276-plus mph. With such a tradition, is it any surprise that a garage in Ormond Beach has become a historic shrine, representing America's "first gasoine alley"? Or that the most influential politician in Daytona is a car salesman?

The mood of the town on the eve of Speed Week, I found when I drove over for the opening of the new Speedway, is one of unalloyed excitement. The excitement gleams in the merchant's eye each time his cash register tinkles; in the motel owner's eye, as he flips on the neon "NO VACANCIES"; in the maiden's eye, as she sees her town suddenly filling with young men of adventurous disposition; and of course in the eye of every civic-minded Daytonan, since his town is about to make its annual splash in newspapers over the country. Everyone cheerfully joins in the promotion. At the restaurant where I lunched there were place mats, special for the occasion, proclaiming Daytona to be the "Speed Capitol (*sic*) of the World!" On every hand there are banners, shouting "Welcome, NASCAR!" which is strange, for the National Association for Stock Car Auto Racing has its headquarters right here in Daytona. It is like watching a man shake hands with himself. In any case, there is no doubt that for this week the town is the nation's acknowledged center of stock-car racing.

There is a tradition that stock-car racing started among the moonshiners, back on the dirt roads that wind around the swamps and pine woods and pot stills of the Carolinas. Commercial considerations, so runs the tale, forced them to come up with cars innocent in appearance—say Ford or Chevrolet or Plymouth sedans—that nevertheless would scoot along when pursued by revenuers as though the Foul Fiend himself had his cloven hoof on the gas. Over the years such powerful cars were developed that outfooting the law became monotonous; to maintain their competitive mettle, the moonshiners got up races among themselves, for a purse, winner take all.

This account undeniably has the ring of truth, especially since the best stock-car racing drivers come from those states —the Carolinas, Georgia, Tennessee, Alabama and Florida— that most engage the attention of the Internal Revenue Service. But today there is an attempt to make the sport respectable, and its official historians recoil from this delightful tradition.

Whatever its origins, stock-car racing got an enormous lift from the explosion of automobile manufacturing that followed the last war. All of a sudden, kids everywhere owned cars and were rebuilding them and driving them, and arguing their competitive merits.

I had thought that the reason stock-car races were so popular was that Death always rode beside the driver. I was swiftly disabused of this notion. It may be that some part of the crowd that turns out at Indianapolis on Memorial Day is there to witness violent death in flames, but this is not the case at Daytona. In any well-conducted stock-car race, the odds are good that there will be an accident, in the sense that a car may roll or plunge out of control; but the odds are overwhelming that no one will be hurt. By far the greatest number of fans at stock-car races have come to root for their favorite to win; and their favorite is not the driver

—although the most successful drivers all have fan clubs. Their favorite is the latest model of American stock car.

It is clear that some measure of subvention must exist even if no one chooses to say precisely how or how much, for to transform an ordinary stock car into a racing machine that will do better than 150 mph is a hideously expensive proposition. How much it can cost was explained to me by a wiry, taciturn man called Smokey Yunick, a racing mechanic who operates a Daytona garage.

When a mechanic like Yunick undertakes to adapt a stock car for racing, he must abide by NASCAR rules which require that a car meet the blueprint specifications of its Detroit designer. These rules are relaxed in a few obvious ways, chiefly for safety's sake. He may brace the body with roll bars; he may add heavy-duty spindles and shock absorbers; he may equip the car with special, eight-ply tires; he may scrap the muffler and clip the exhaust pipe; most important, he may install any sort of camshaft, for to check a camshaft against the blueprint would take NASCAR's inspectors far more time than they have available.

But there is another, even more salient difference. The mechanic takes the car completely apart and puts it back together again, in the process endowing the engine with optimum performance tolerances. In short, what was a relatively crude assembly-line product becomes, in his hands, a machine precisely fitted by a craftsman. Yunick estimates that 2000 man-hours are needed to do the job. And what had a price tag of $2500 is now worth $15,000.

No question about it, Detroit approves of such expenditures. It is the industry's way of insuring that here at Daytona its product will reign as queen. And her throne is the new, handsome Speedway.

I got my first look at the racetrack designed to keep Daytona in the big league of automotive speed late on the afternoon before its formal opening. Access is through a tunnel to the infield, so that you get a sudden, unexpected view of the whole sweep of the track. A dozen cars were buzzing around in practice runs, like angry hornets. My eye was caught by one car—it was painted a raucous red—and even from the basin of the infield I could follow it around the entire two and a half miles. Visually the most exciting features are the wide, deep, sharply banked turns at either end: as the cars race 2700 feet across them, you see only their tops making shifting patterns, like blobs of color seen in a jumbo kaleidoscope.

The red car was zipping along (I had my stop watch on it) at about 130 mph, and when presently it slowed down to approach the pit area I was even more impressed. For, aside from its coat of alarming paint, it looked like a rather dowdy Ford sedan, at least 15 years old. It was in fact a 1940 Ford, but magic had been worked under its hood.

Behind the wheel was a grizzled, gentle-voiced man in his forties. He was Lee Petty, a North Carolina farmer, old enough to have a son who was also to race over the weekend. His venerable Ford, almost as old as his son, was classified under NASCAR regulations as "modified"—which means that its owner may have done almost anything to its engine short of equipping it with rocket propulsion—and it was entered in a race limited to other such "modified" marvels. A less glamorous entry for a sports event would have been difficult to imagine.

Indeed, there seems to be a conspiracy to make *all* the entries in a stock-car race as ugly as possible. Once a car has been converted into a superb racing machine, it is apparently handed over to a spray-gun painter who confuses esthetics with hysteria. Nearly are all daubed with shrill, electric colors and further defaced by advertising matter. Every color except green is used; superstition has outlawed green (as it has also outlawed, for obscure reasons, the eating of peanuts from the shell anywhere near a driver on the day of a race; if you would like to collect on your insurance, don a green shirt and eat some peanuts in the pit area on the Sunday of Speed Week).

The effect of all this dubious decoration is to make the cars look like taxicabs. Evidently nobody cares, though, except me and a man named James Stephens, whose Pontiac was painted a glossy black, with a minimum of advertising. His was easily the handsomest automobile in the year's big race and, driven by a local Daytona hero, Glen (Fireball) Roberts, even held an early lead for a few laps. I imagine Mr. Stephens agreed with me that the race lost much of its elegance when engine trouble forced his entry to withdraw.

The garage area, on the eve of the weekend's racing, is in a state of controlled confusion. Mechanics are busy with spot welder and wrench. One youngster, a Texan called Shorty Rollins, whose engine had blown earlier that day, was feverishly installing another one in his convertible, which was entered in the next day's race. (In the finest celluloid tradition, Rollins won.) At sundown these last-minute check-ups were interrupted when a voice on a public-address system summoned all the drivers to a meeting.

If their cars lack a certain chic, the same is true of the drivers. The half-a-hundred men who gathered for the drivers' meeting had rejected any temptation to look like the trained athletes they must be. Not glamour, they seemed to have agreed, but utility should be the keynote. In their windbreakers and greasy coveralls they looked like men lounging around in Gasoline Alley. And yet it was not hard to imagine these same men as pilots of the Strategic Air Command, being briefed for a critical mission: they are of the breed.

The meeting had been called by the genial, outsize promoter, Bill France, who is president both of NASCAR and of the Speedway. After a few perfunctory remarks about safety in the next day's races, France introduced the men who had helped finance the Speedway (except for the principal angel, Clint Murchison, Jr., the Texas rich man, who hadn't yet arrived). Then the meeting broke up, and all hands began to look for a party.

Parties blossom all over the Halifax area toward the end of Speed Week. Some are large and well-behaved, some are small and well-behaved, and some are small. Most are expressions of Daytona hospitality to the visiting politicians, the Army and Air Force and Navy brass, and the Detroit executives, together with such show-business personalities as are automotive fans. And some, more exclusive, are annual reunions of old friends, for the same faces are likely to be seen year after year during Speed Week. One of the drivers, better-heeled than most, throws a party every year in his motel suite. That year he arrived to find the suite had been redecorated in his honor—in green. His party started on schedule, his knowledgeable guests ignoring the reek of fresh *green* paint.

But for the dedicated automotive man there is no time for parties. Morning after morning he has a date on the beach for the Century Club runs; in the afternoon there are the time trials and races at the Speedway; and at night, in the Daytona Stadium, there are the midget-car races. What buff can afford to miss any of these events? And yet, rousing as these excitements are to the motor fans from Ohio and New York and Oklahoma and Illinois who have carefully planned that their vacations shall coincide with

137

Speed Week, they are nothing compared with the Sunday sweepstakes. For here, annually, the stock car is apotheosized.

Outside the speedway, handling traffic on the big day, is what seems to be the entire National Guard; over the highways for miles around hover helicopters, guiding the latecomers; blimps float above the track; through the ether the voices of four radio announcers carry word of the great event over a hookup of small stations to those fans in the southeastern states who didn't have gas money to attend in person; in the grandstands, in seats scaled up to 20 dollars, sit the quality; but the dedicated automotive man is in the infield, and it is there that you get the undiluted flavor of Speed Week.

What goes on in the infield at Daytona Beach cannot, to be sure, be compared with the activities at a racetrack like that in Darlington, S.C., where mountaineers arrive in their thousands on the eve of the Labor Day "Southern 500" to dance all night to country fiddles. There is a drunk-tank in the middle of the Darlington Raceway, so I have been told, for the convenience of the local police who are, for the occasion, clad in Confederate gray.

Watching a race that lasts nearly four hours under a hot sun calls for fortitude. The start is exciting: 60-odd cars, in two rows, paced around the track at 75 mph, until down goes the flag and away they roar, at 100, 125, 150 mph, into the west turn, scrambling and butting and shoving each other for headway; but quite soon they have settled down to a monotonous grind; and before long even the official scorer would be puzzled, at any given moment as to whether a certain car is sixth or sixtieth. To be sure, something may happen: an engine may blow, a car may turn over and over, careening crazily into the fence; but it usually happens a mile away. No matter: still the automotive man sits in the sun, watching the cars whirl past, fascinated hour after hour by their hypnotic whine. He is supremely happy.

A fat man stretches out half-naked on the roof of his car, sunbathing; two college kids, who have driven a day and a night to get here, curl up in their car and doze; chin-whiskered mountaineers stroll about, wearing cowboy boots and tiny black souvenir derbies; a man who has equipped himself with a step-ladder and a pair of binoculars perches six feet atop his car, scanning the horizon, while below in the grass his wife reads *True Romance*. And so the hours pass.

The spectators have not even a financial interest to sustain them. Despite the certainty each feels that the winner will be Ford, Plymouth or Chevrolet, or Pontiac, De Soto or Oldsmobile, I did not see a solitary bookmaker who would profit from all this enthusiasm. A tragic commentary on the decline of private enterprise.

Perhaps, then, the fans' interest is kept alive by the hope of a thrilling finish? But in a 500-mile race the winner is almost always a certainty for the last 20 laps, and usually he has outdistanced his rivals by two or three miles.

And yet that year, as if to confound tradition, the gods smiled on the Speedway and provided it with the most exhilarating race in automotive history. Not only those in the infield, not only those in the grandstands, even those sitting at home listening to the radio were electrified as for the last 50 miles a 1959 Oldsmobile and a 1959 Ford Thunderbird whirled around lap after lap never more than a few feet apart. The finish was unprecedented. It required a camera, but of course none had been provided, for no one had anticipated the need. Meantime, all over the racecourse 47,000 voices were raised in exultation for a victor who had averaged 135.521 mph for 500 miles—a speed exceeded only fractionally even by the Indianapolis-type racing cars.

But which car was the victor? Most of those who had seen the finish agreed that it was the Oldsmobile (and so did I, if for no other reason than that the Oldsmobile had been driven by Lee Petty, the veteran whose "modified" Ford had caught my eye three days before); yet the race officials declared the Thunderbird had triumphed. And it was three days before newspaper photographs of the finish caused them to reverse their decision.

Such a finish, and such a speed, the automotive experts present agreed, could have come only on such an exceedingly fast track. And then the automotive experts set about coping with the immediate realities of automotive travel, which involved trying to cover the five miles back to Daytona Beach in less than an hour.

Speed Week proved a bonanza for Daytona Beach, and this year and the next and the next will bring even more delectable profits. The stunning success of Bill France's Speedway makes this a certainty.

RACING IS A VICE

by Alfonso De Portago

Every five years or so a racing driver, no better nor worse than the others, springs magically into the international limelight. Usually his personality overshadows his accomplishments; he is cursed, blessed, spat upon, beloved. Such drivers were Barney Oldfield, Mike Hawthorn, and Jean Behra. Such a driver too, was Don Alfonso Cabeza de Vaca y Leighton, the 17th Marquis de Portago. Beginning with no driving skill (though already an expert horseman, bobsledder, and lover), cars were nothing to him—except the means of achieving a deep ambition. What that ambition was, and what led him to his tragic end, may be seen in his last article, which ran in the pages of **Sports Illustrated** just a few days prior to his death. It is followed by a postscript from the same magazine, written by William Rospigliosi who reported Portago's last ride.

What type of man becomes a professional racing driver? At heart he must be an adventurer. Six hundred years ago he would have been off to the Crusades or would have more conservatively stayed at home, slain a few dragons and have saved an occasional damsel in distress. Today, however, the Crusades are over, the dragons are in hiding, and if a damsel gets in trouble she calls the police or her psychiatrist.

Adventure is a religion. Religions require faith, and the adventurer must above all other things have faith in himself. It is the uncertainty of the future that attracts the adventurer most. Few professions, except possibly that of Communist politics, have less security and more uncertainty about the future than racing. One can be at the top one second, but all it requires is one very small error and one is very embarrassingly dead the next.

As one may well imagine, racing is an extremely competitive business. In most sports today, the old spirit of "the game for the game's sake" is fast dying out, and with the exception of a few isolated outposts of the British Empire and, naturally, the playing fields of Eton and Harrow, everyone has acquired a somewhat deplorable desire to win. However, as we approach the limits of human and mechanical ability, it accordingly becomes increasingly difficult, both mentally and physically, to surmount the actual records.

Speed is the keynote of our age. But the sportsman who has neither the physical ability to run a four- or even five-minute mile nor the mental ability to work on things like guided missiles has to settle for such sports as automobile racing and bobsledding. Both of these occupations also have the advantage that one remains, at least most of the time, in a comfortable, seated position. There is none of this nonsense of running around the park at some ungodly hour to keep in proper trim. As we race every Sunday from March to October, after the initial month's racing we automatically (and much to our surprise) find ourselves in excellent shape. We then are able with little or no effort to maintain this condition to the season's end. It is very definitely one of the prime requisites of being a good driver to have, first, the physical strength to drive a car at very high speeds for at least three hours in what is practically unbearable heat, as, for example, in Argentina, and second to have the mental strength to be able to concentrate upon one's driving for the same length of time.

Are we brave? Not necessarily. An act of courage is the performance of an act in which one overcomes fear. Driving a car at what most people would consider a suicidal speed is not frightening to us. We have spent many years learning how to do so with a minimum of risk. At times a driver will perform an act of courage, such as going off the road in preference to hitting a spectator. The mere fact that we race requires no courage on our part. To put it in a nutshell, we are not brave because as far as automobile racing is concerned we have no fear to overcome.

But do we ever get frightened? We get terrified. Fear is the awareness of danger. Whenever a driver makes a mistake and loses control of his car for even a split second, the danger is acute and he is frightened. However, he knows what he should do to rectify his mistake (if it is reparable), so his fear is, in most cases, of very short duration and is quickly forgotten. On the other hand, if the mistake is a serious one, it always seems like an eternity between the time one loses control of the car until the time one hits whatever one is going to hit. I, myself, am considered quite an expert on the subject of going off the road. I have never enjoyed doing so, even at slow speeds. I think what frightens me most is that when I have actually lost control of the car there is absolutely nothing I can do except sit still, frozen with fear, and wait for events to take their natural course.

A driver's first feeling when he goes off the road and is unhurt is one of shame. All the way back to the pits he will be busy concocting a reasonable excuse. I have heard the most extraordinary stories about a new species of tree that will actually jump out into the road and hit cars with considerable violence. Most drivers, however, stick to simple little tales of small children and/or old women crossing the road in front of them.

The problem of automobile racing is not one of winning at the highest possible speed but rather one of winning at the lowest possible speed. Fangio has been practicing this theory with rather more than a modicum of success for some years now. It is obvious that the slower one goes the less chance there is of breaking down. At the same time, however, one must go fast enough to be the first car across the finish line. Fangio more often wins races by 10 seconds than by five minutes, and he does this by preference.

In the Grand Prix of Cuba, which is run over a distance of 320 miles, I knew that Fangio was very worried whether his brakes would last the entire race. I knew that the best chance I would have of beating him would be to force him to use his brakes as hard as possible. This strategy worked for a while. Fangio, after briefly trying to pass me, let me go ahead by myself. After we had both made our pit stops to refuel on about the 55th lap, I was ahead by about 65 seconds. My car was not only running perfectly but my brakes were in good condition. I hadn't a worry in the world.

On the 65th lap I happened to see Fangio coming down one straight as I was going up the other. I probably saw his face for half a second. The expression on it gave me a terrible shock. He was completely relaxed and unworried. He had the expression of a man who *knew* that he was shortly going to win the Grand Prix of Cuba. Five laps later a gas line on my car broke. I was forced to come into the pits. It took my mechanics five minutes to repair it. When I rejoined the race, I was in sixth position, with Fangio, naturally, in first. I eventually managed to finish third (and

142

establish the lap record). But as long as I live I shall never forget that glimpse I got of Fangio's face.

I think that the hardest part of racing is the start of a driver's career. He is more or less forced to take chances to draw attention to himself and prove to the car manufacturers his potentialities for the future. If he can stay alive and in one piece for the first couple of years, this is half the battle. If he is fortunate to possess financial resources of his own, he will have to buy at least one car a year. The car will cost him from $6,000 to $15,000 and naturally never go quite as fast as the factory cars he has to compete against. The time he loses going down the straights he will have to try and make up on braking and in the corners. Since he is competing against the best drivers in the world, if our young driver can even pass the fourth car on any works team he is really showing great ability.

Once the driver has been noticed by a racing director his next step will be to drive a works car in one of the major sports car races and, what is more important, to finish in it—even in 27th position. What the racing director will neither forgive nor forget is the young driver who goes off the road or who breaks his engine by overrevving it. One must not forget that in the world of motor racing the racing directors, men like Enzo Ferrari, Orsi of Maserati, Lyons of Jaguar, etc., are the prophets of the gods.

Early last year I had a friend ask Enzo Ferrari why, despite the fact that I was driving quite fast, I was not on his team. His answer arrived a few days later in a large envelope. It contained two pictures of myself going off the road the previous Sunday at the Nürburgring. Not very subtle perhaps, but brief and to the point. Fortunately for me, Luigi Musso broke his arm during the same race, and as Ferrari needed a fourth driver he forgave me, and since then I have been a member of the Ferrari team.

Automobile racing is one of the cleanest sports in the world—especially Grand Prix racing, where only the best professionals compete. Perhaps the reason it is clean is that it is very effectively self-policed. If someone is unkind to me in a race today, I have two possible solutions for dealing with him. I can wait until I next lap him or he laps me, or I can more patiently wait until the following Sunday, when we meet again. And if revenge is sweet, it is only sweet for the avenger. This, however, very rarely occurs as all the drivers are very close friends; so, if two drivers have a lovers' spat, it is usually of very brief duration. It must be remembered that we spend four days a week together from March to October, and we all know each other's little problems, both foreign and domestic. Shortly after the finish of a race everyone disappears without saying goodby. The following Thursday conversations and poker games are resumed where they left off, as if there had been no interruption. On the whole, drivers are, I think, a very happy lot and suffer from very few neuroses. Perhaps we appreciate life more because we live closer to death.

Racing is a vice, and as such extremely hard to give up. All drivers swear that they will stop at such and such an age, but very few of them are able to do so. Racing drivers are inveterate gamblers and, like most of the breed, never know when to stop. Sometimes when a friend is killed you swear that you will never race again. The next day you think, well, this could never happen to me. By the third day you've got your gear together and you are off to the next race.

The art of racing is primarily a matter of sensitivity. Every curve or corner has a theoretical maximum speed. The closer one can approach this maximum the faster one goes. This sensitivity is neither in one's hands, one's head or one's feet, but in the seat of one's pants. When a car is trying, as we call it, to break loose, we feel it in the seat of our pants and nowhere else. This is probably the least romantic aspect of motor racing, but it is so.

The greatest difficulty a driver encounters and the true test of his ability is what we call "a fast curve." This means we come down a straight at speeds up to 160 mph and then have to take a curve whose maximum speed is, say, 130 mph. What makes Fangio Fangio is that he will take this curve at 129.9, when another driver will take it at 125 or at 130.1—in which case he will go off the road.

Where does a driver get this sensitivity? He can be born with it. Then he can develop it further by many other sports, the best of which is probably horseback riding. Moss, Collins and I all used to ride a great deal, principally in races. I eventually started putting on weight, and although I tried all the known systems of slimming it was all to no avail. So that was the end of my riding career. In motor racing, weight is of far less importance. The manufacturers will go to extreme lengths to save a few pounds here and there.

However, this does not seem to prevent Fangio, who is probably the heaviest driver, from also being the fastest.

The most thankless task in our world is no doubt that of the mechanic. He will frequently have to work throughout the night to get a car ready, or to change an axle ratio. The driver will then get into the car, do a few laps and come back into the pits complaining that the car isn't going well. This, of course, will necessitate another night's work for the mechanic. Fortunately, mechanics seem to accept this as part of the cross they have to bear. When their car wins, they are just as proud and pleased as the driver, despite the fact that they get absolutely no recognition for the part they have played.

Automobile racing is dangerous, but it is only as dangerous as you want to make it. Ninety percent of all accidents are directly due to drivers' mistakes—not necessarily those of the driver who has the accident, but all too frequently (especially in sports car races) due to inexperienced drivers. They are the greatest menace of all to the faster men. Once a fast driver has committed himself to a certain line in a fast curve, he can no longer change it, or, once in the curve, apply his brakes. If somebody else, who is going slower, does change his line, there is inevitably going to be a mixup.

Another 5% of the accidents are caused by mechanical failures, steering arms breaking, rear ends locking, tires blowing, etc. The remaining 5% are the public's fault. The vast majority of the spectators prefer to stand in what they consider the most likely place for an accident to occur and, of course, they will think nothing of strolling across the course if they so desire. Sometimes they stroll at the wrong time and in the wrong place.

The closest escape I have ever had occurred last year at Le Mans during practice. My co-driver was Duncan Hamilton, who had already won at Le Mans. I always like to have a Thermos of water in my car so that I may have an occasional sip (through a rubber tube) if and when I so desire. Duncan, however, does not care for water and had substituted my Thermos for one of his own filled with a revolting recipe of his which is, I believe, 70% champagne to 30% brandy. He had, somewhat thoughtlessly, forgotten to mention this to me. I am a teetotaler and detest even the taste of wine. After two or three laps of practice I felt slightly thirsty and inserted my trusty rubber tube in my mouth, drew in a full mouthful of Duncan's foul concoction and swallowed it before I realized what I had done. At the time I was on the Mulsanne straight and cruising along at 160 mph. The top of my head seemed to fly off. I couldn't see where I was going. The five or six following seconds were, as Duncan would say, extremely dicey. In the race itself, a 24-hour affair, two Jaguars spun directly in front of me on the second lap. I crashed into them, putting all three cars out of the race. I, of course, blamed my hangover.

Racing drivers, all of them, are terribly nervous before a race. Some of them show it more than others. But if you ever see a driver looking calm and relaxed 10 minutes before the start of a race, believe me, it's all a big act. Once the race is started, however, we all resemble the legendary cucumber.

I still think that it is safer to drive in a Grand Prix and far less strain on one's nerves than it is to drive from Paris to the Riviera during the summer months, or in this country during the Fourth of July weekend.

POSTSCRIPT: DEATH AT GUIDIZZOLO

by William Rospigliosi

Dateline: May 19, 1957. They called him *uno simpaticone*. They were with him. The loudspeakers said he had passed Mantua, passed Goito and was on the straight stretch between Goito and Guidizzolo. The people waited, but he did not appear.

Portago had driven a hard race. He would not have driven at all, for it is a race much hated by most of the drivers, but young Cesare Perdisa gave up racing after the recent death of the Italian champion, Eugenio Castellotti, and Portago, as a member of the Ferrari team, was asked to take Perdisa's 3.8 Ferrari. Reluctantly, with a premonition of disaster that he communicated to a few friends, he did. Even after Perdisa's withdrawal (to become a horseman), Portago might have bypassed the race. The talented Luigi Musso might have taken the car, but he became sick. . . . Portago had actually never been round the entire Mille Miglia course, though he had twice attempted it. The first time, Portago's car had caught fire at Ferrara, and the second time out he had run into a mile-stone almost at the start of the course.

It is a tribute to his skill and daring that he kept to fourth place the whole way, despite this very grave handicap. In the best tradition of the Romantic, Portago had interrupted his rush toward Brescia, near Rome, upon seeing his frequent companion of late, the movie actress Linda Christian. He had stopped his car, waited for the actress to run to him, then had lifted her up and kissed her before roaring onward. . . .

After 550 miles of running, came the hairpin bend northward—the bend which joins the Flaminian and the Cassian ways. Collins took it perfectly—right in the center of the road—in a smooth arc with no wheel screech. Taruffi, in his customary black overalls and silver helmet, swung wide before the bend and, calmly with upraised head, took the road that led him north to victory. But Portago's lack of knowledge

147

of the route was very apparent when he took the bend too fast, seemed suddenly surprised to find it was a hairpin and, with the car straining outward, only just managed to complete the turn.

Handicapped by this lack of experience in the thousands of turns of Italy's narrow, sinuous roads, Portago drove harder than most, attempting to win by sheer virtuosity. He had only 30 miles to go—a few minutes left to drive—when it happened. The narrow bridge of Goito was behind him, the tormenting twists of the Apennines forgotten, and the inviting tape of the road through the Po Valley lay before him.

The spectators who lined the road saw him coming—first a dot in the distance, looming larger every second. He must have been going 150 mph. Children tried to force themselves past the legs of their elders, up to the front of the crowd. There was a sudden report, followed by a hiss—a tire blowing out—and the dot that was Portago, a red Ferrari by now, swerved violently. Its tail hit the bank at the left of the road. Then the car catapulted above the first line of onlookers, cut the telegraph wires above, and landed among the more timorous spectators who had stayed back for greater safety. Amid the shrieks of the injured and dying, Portago died immediately, and with him his old friend, the American Edmund Nelson, who had come along for the ride.

GENTLE JIMMY

by John Tomerlin

Capable racing drivers who are also capable writers are rare. Included in this especially-talented group are John Fitch, Sammy Davis, Paul Frere and perhaps two or three others. Certainly, one can also add John Tomerlin. Although, unlike the others, he has never had a truly dramatic, first-rate machine at his disposal, he has nonetheless acquitted himself, on numerous demanding circuits, with considerable distinction, often besting cars of far greater potential. Just as impressive are his victories in the writing category, where he has been cited as a talented writer of fiction and nonfiction.

They called them the Roaring Twenties, and roar they did with the get-rich roar of Wall Street tycoons, the alcoholic roar of Prohibition and, loudest of all, the thundering engine roar of Racing's Golden Age. America was in love with speed and progress, and the automobile was a symbol of both. National eminence was tested on the race tracks of the world, where for too many years the great teams of Italy and England had reigned supreme. Now, as if in answer to a call, a new alloy of men and machines boiled out of our nation's melting pot—drivers like Rickenbacker, DePalma, Cooper, Milton and Chevrolet; in cars built by Duesenberg, Frontenac, Miller and Durant—new heroes of a dazzling decade. To their grateful public, these men were the giants who carried America's pride wheel-high into combat. And for five brief years, no giant stood taller than a five-foot-seven-inch, 145-pound Irishman named James Anthony Murphy.

In the short span allotted him, Murphy did more for American prestige than any driver before or since. He captured world records for the United States, helped end foreign domination of the Indianapolis Speedway Classic, and carried the battle to Europe soil where he had won the Grand Prix of France. That he was one of the greatest drivers of all

149

time is a matter of record. He won the first championship race he ever drove, added 17 more and two national titles to his record, and compiled the fifth highest total of championship points in history; a performance that has never been equalled in a comparable period of time. He was a national hero, the most popular figure of his day. They named a dance after him, the Jimmy Murphy Fox Trot, and he was mourned like a matinee idol at his death in 1924. Yet more remarkable than all this, perhaps, is the fact that today he is hardly remembered. Men with no more ability—many of them with less—became legends and their names remain fresh in memory. But Murphy died as he had lived, pursuing his private god of speed, was buried, and was forgotten by all but the statisticians.

This is a mystery . . . that a man could accomplish so much, and leave so little trace of himself behind. Those who knew him, who are still alive, shed no light on the matter. "He was a nice fellow," they say, "everybody liked him." Indeed, everybody liked him: the public, his fellow drivers, mechanics, movie stars and chiefs of state. It becomes a sort of a shield, this likeability, behind which the real man hides (for, of course, it is easier to "like" someone you do not know than to hate him), and this is at the heart of the problem. No one ever really *knew* Jimmy Murphy.

He was born in 1894, in San Francisco, and was an orphan at the age of 10. He never knew his mother, and the shock of his father's death (in the San Francisco earthquake) left him a guarded and taciturn child. He went to live with relatives —the Judge and Mrs. Martin O'Donnell—in Vernon, California, and later attended Huntington Park High School where he proved too small for sports and too shy to make friends. Only one significant event marked this period of his life. Judge O'Donnell bought him a motorcycle to drive to and from school, and thus unlocked the one great talent in Jimmy's life: his genius for things mechanical. At the end of his junior year, Murphy quit school to open a small garage at the corner of what are now Washington and Main Streets in downtown Los Angeles. At about this time, also, he began spending free afternoons at the nearby Beverly Speedway.

The Beverly Speedway! Something inside Jimmy responded to the spectacle of racing in the early 1900s. How could it have been otherwise? His heart beat faster at the exploits of men like Bob Burman, Eddie Hearne, Ray Harroun and Teddy (The Terrible) Tetzlaff. He watched the mechanics in the pits—men with awesome names stitched across their coveralls—as they lavished care on the bright-colored thunder-throated machines that meant wealth and glory, and he thought to himself: "I could do that."

The cars of the day were high, heavy, unreliable brutes requiring two strong men to handle them. The best of the breed was the great Duesenberg team with drivers like Eddie O'Donnell, Tommy Milton, Eddie Hearne and Eddie (not then Captain) Rickenbacker. They were, to racing, what the New York Yankees have become to baseball. Every man who raced dreamed of the day he might race with Duesenberg, and it was with this team that Jimmy got his start.

The place was Corona, California, the year 1916. After months of watching and waiting, Murphy had finally been offered a job as riding mechanic with a driver named Omar Taft. On the morning of the race, however, Taft's car was disqualified, and Jimmy was sitting disconsolately on a stack of spare tires when Eddie O'Donnell happened by. "What's the matter, kid?" the veteran driver asked, and Jimmy told him what had happened. O'Donnell looked thoughtful. "Matter of fact, my mechanic is laid up today. How'd you like to ride with me?"

Ride with O'Donnell? In a Duesenberg?

("How'd you like the pot of gold at the end of the rainbow . . . the key to Shangri-La . . . the most beautiful girl in the world . . . ?") Three hundred and one miles later a Duesenberg flashed first across the finish line, and the winning driver turned to his breathless mechanic.

"Pack your bags, kid. You've got yourself a job."

During the next three years he rode with O'Donnell, Milton and Rickenbacker; he served his apprenticeship well, and near the end of the 1919 season he got the break he'd been waiting for: his first chance behind the wheel. It was nearly his last. He crashed at Uniontown, injuring his co-rider, Lyle Jolls, and convincing Fred Duesenberg that Murphy would never be anything more than a good mechanic.

Tommy Milton disagreed. Milton was, by this time, the number one driver on the team and destined to become one of racing's immortals. He was close-mouthed, quick-tempered, and had few friends, but his mechanic was one of them and he had made up his mind that Jimmy should have another chance. "Either he drives again, or I leave the team," he told Duesenberg flatly, and when an arm injury sidelined O'Donnell before the 1920 curtain-raiser at Beverly Speedway, Jimmy got the nod. Milton had had his way, and he must have remembered the incident with bitterness in later years. For he alone came to hate the man that "everybody liked."

The Beverly race ushered in what students of the sport have called the greatest age of auto racing in America's history, and with it came the "Era of Wonderful Nonsense" —the 20s. Capacity crowds turned out to watch the noisy, flamboyant, often deadly carnivals of speed that took place on the board tracks of Altoona, Uniontown, Beverly Hills and Sheepshead Bay. The quickly-forgotten names of America's war heroes were replaced by the soon-to-be-forgotten names of men like Harry Hartz, Eddie Miller, Roscoe Sarles, Howard Wilcox—and Jimmy Murphy.

Not that anyone paid the slightest attention that first day to the little Irishman propped up in O'Donnell's seat, straining to see over the high cowling. But when qualifying times were announced, the crowd was stunned to hear that a man driving in his first full race had won the pole position. Before the shock had worn off, the starter's flag fell and Murphy thundered into the lead. "My God," Fred Duesenberg cried, turning away from the spectacle. "I thought he'd learned his lesson at Uniontown!"

Apparently he had. Murphy was never headed over the 250 miles, winning at a new record speed and drawing away on every lap from men like Joe Boyer, Cliff Durant, Ralph Mulford, Ira Vail and Ralph DePalma. On his "cool off" lap, having taken the checkered flag, he ran out of gas and had to be pushed to the pits. "Talk about breaks," one of the drivers mumbled, "that guy's got the luck of the Irish."

If it was luck, Murphy's leprechaun proceeded to run wild. He won again at Fresno (where his back axle was found hanging together by a single thread of the last nut, after all the other cars on the team had failed), finished second in two races at Uniontown, third at Elgin, fourth at Indianapolis and sixth at Tacoma, narrowly missing the National Championship. Near the end of the season, he broke the existing land speed record at Daytona Beach to complete what is probably the most amazing rookie year in the annals of any sport. It was the Daytona run, however, that cost him Milton's friendship and started one of the most publicized feuds in racing.

Duesenberg had prepared a super-powered car to try for the mark then held by Ralph DePalma, and Milton was scheduled to drive it on his return from a race in Havana. For some reason, Duesenberg decided to send Jimmy down to conduct "trials," and the record was promptly shattered at 151 miles per hour. Milton was on the boat back from Cuba when he heard about it. He was enraged. The honor of breaking the mark held by DePalma—another bitter rival—was one he had looked forward to, and, as top team driver, he was entitled to it. He eventually did set a new mark with the car, but this failed to heal the wound Murphy had inflicted. "I designed most of that car myself," Milton said. "I welded the frame rails, formed out the body panels, and spent a lot of my own money to build it. Then a kid comes along who I *started* in this business, and breaks the record with it!"

Milton's testimony must be taken seriously, for he knew Murphy as well as any man ever did, and he'd glimpsed a side of the young Irishman that few others saw: a terrible need, behind his smiling friendly facade, to win, to be the best, to find an identity that would prove he was "someone" —not just an orphan boy who had never been any good at sports, but *Jimmy Murphy*, the greatest racing driver of them all.

It was a baseball manager who said, "Nice guys finish last," and the aphorism could apply even more accurately to the dog-eat-dog world of motor racing. Yet, to most people, there never was a nicer guy than Murphy, nor one who finished first more regularly. As a driver he had two great assets: an uncanny mechanical instinct, which told him exactly how much strain his own and other drivers' cars would stand, and a monumental calm behind the wheel. Murphy took no unnecessary chances on the track; he preferred to let someone else lead the race if challenged—and if certain the other driver's car would not stand the pace. It was as though he had told himself, "Sure, it's a dangerous sport, and the only one I'm any good at . . . but why risk more than I have to?"

In this respect, as in most others, he was unlike his counterparts of that era. Barney Oldfield had left an indelible image on the public mind as to what a racing figure ought to be: hard-drinking, hard-living, hard-playing—the expected rewards of a tenuous existence—and most drivers tried hard to live up to expectations. They gambled away their winnings on the trains that carried them from one arena to another, and bragged openly to the press in conscious or unconscious imitation of the cigar-chewing "King of Speed," Oldfield. Murphy was a notable exception to all of this. "It isn't what I *say* I'll do that counts," he would tell copy-hungry reporters. "They only pay me for where I actually finish."

He finished well enough to earn over $130,000 in 1922 alone—and kept most of it in a day when income taxes were negligible. He stayed out of the Pullman-aisle crap games, and appeared to have no special tastes in either food or clothing, factors which contributed to his reputation for being "unspoiled by success." The truth, however, is that Murphy did not like to spend money. He was, in the words of his teammate, Ernie Miller, "the most conservative man I ever knew." Miller remembers an evening spent with Murphy, several of the other drivers and their wives. They had dined out, and "somewhere along the way Jimmy lost a ten-dollar bill. He couldn't get over it. It ended up pretty much spoiling the evening for all of us."

Yet it would be wrong to conclude that Murphy did not get what he wanted out of life. He was, after all, 10 years old before he found a safe and permanent home, old enough to have formed a fear of rootlessness and insecurity sufficient to drive him all of his days. He must have looked back along the road he'd traveled from time to time and realized that no young man from the farm had ever dreamed brighter dreams and seen them come true. It must have been reward enough for anything he felt life had denied him.

Murphy broke from his cautious pattern of living—and driving—only twice during his career. Once, to get out of a hospital bed for a race he wanted very much to win, and once to drive a race he wanted very much to avoid. The first brought him his most lasting fame; the second cost him his life.

In 1921, Albert Champion, the spark plug manufacturer and a native of France, decided that it was time for the United States to be represented abroad. Consequently, he arranged to pay transportation and entry for a team of Duesenbergs at the Grand Prix at Le Mans. The cars, having just run at Indianapolis, had to be shipped over in parts and assembled before the race, and the French can be excused for considering them a rather amusing sidelight to the race. The sleek blue Ballots, one of which was being driven by Ralph DePalma, were certain to win.

Murphy made the trip with a seriously burned right hand, and ran into nothing but bad luck from the time he arrived. A week before the race he went out to test a new set of brakes. They locked up on him, causing him to lose control of the car and plunge off the road. A small ditch tossed him out of the cockpit, and he fractured several ribs in landing. The car was repaired quickly enough, but Murphy himself ended up in the hospital. On the morning of the race, Ernie Olson and a nurse applied tape from just below his armpits to his hips, and he was driven out to the track and lifted into his car. What followed must rank as a high mark of human courage.

The road surface was bad to begin with, and after a few laps began to disintegrate completely. Every inch of each eight-mile lap became an agony for Murphy. Rocks the size of tennis balls were hurled from beneath the tires of cars, into those behind. "Every time we went to pass someone," Olson says, "I'd reach out and jerk up a screen we'd made out of wire mesh. It sounded like we were being strafed with a machine gun!" Two laps from the finish, a stone pierced the Duesenberg's radiator, and the engine began to smoke. A lap later and a tire burst. They were leading the race, several minutes ahead of DePalma, and Murphy was afraid to stop for fear of stalling the by-now red hot engine. As the American car staggered across the finish line, the first sight that greeted Murphy and Olson was the French color guard—waiting in *DePalma's* pit. "They couldn't believe we'd made it," Olson says, "but we had."

Considering the pain Murphy withstood, and the chances he took in this event, it becomes necessary to re-examine the modest, mild-mannered Irishman. Clearly there was nothing casual in his racing, and just as clearly he was motivated by forces as strong as those felt by any of his contemporaries. Moreover, he continued to race after he'd reached all his declared objectives. He had won a European Grand Prix (it would be 40 years before an American won another); he had won Indianapolis; he had won the National Championship in 1922; he had said he'd quit, time and again. But he didn't. He narrowly missed another national title in 1923, then ran off with everything in sight the following year. Even then, he showed no real inclination to step out of the limelight. Viewed from this angle, the end seems to have been almost inevitable. It came in 1924.

Syracuse was the next-to-last event of the season, and with the championship well in hand, Murphy had planned to pass it up. He had never liked dirt tracks; control was too unsure, the surface too changeable for his steady style. But he had been told that his championship might be jeopardized if he held out, so he filed an entry. "Wag" Wagner tells of what happened:

"Jimmy wasn't terribly superstitious, as many of the drivers are. He wore a St. Christopher's medal, but he was a devout Catholic so this wasn't unusual. He did share one taboo with the others, though; he disliked making travel arrangements in advance of a race. The afternoon of Syracuse, I went over to Jimmy's pit and gave him his train tickets for the trip home. He asked me to keep them, but I had an engagement right after the race and was afraid I wouldn't see him in time. I tucked the tickets in his breast pocket. Afterwards, I often wondered about this . . ."

It happened near the end of the race, as Murphy was moving up to take the lead. His tires touched an oil spot, and the car began to slide toward the inside rail. It was not a bad accident as such things go; Milton had walked away from an almost identical one, at the same track, about a week before. But this time a splinter of the wooden stringer tore loose and pierced the driver's heart. Jimmy Murphy was dead at the age of 30.

It's interesting to note that Tommy Milton accompanied the body back to Los Angeles and made most of the funeral arrangements. In the end, apparently even he could not hold a grudge against gentle Jimmy. He had fought him on the track—as Milton fought everyone—but perhaps his heart had not been in it. Perhaps he regretted that Jimmy never took the feud very seriously; had never answered his attacks in the newspapers; had never battled him hub-to-hub for the victories that seemed to come so naturally to the younger man. Perhaps he wished he had known Murphy really well, so that he could have hated him—or loved him—more strongly. But he didn't know him. No one ever did. No one ever will.

MICKEY THOMPSON: RECORDBREAKER

by Wayne Thoms

At this writing, Marion Lee "Mickey" Thompson's national and international speed records total 186, encompassing marks in 16 separate classes—more categories than any individual has ever taken. Here is the tense, on-the-scene story of two of those record assaults as related by Wayne Thoms, one of our best automotive writers, who was there when Mickey hit the throttle.

Mickey Thompson quietly slid behind the wheel of a blue Pontiac Catalina sedan at 6:30 A.M. on July 15th, 1962, drove casually away from a small group of people with whom he had been talking, picked a starting point, and immediately roared out of sight through heavy dawn mists along the main runway of March Air Force Base. Almost before anyone was aware of what had happened, he sped back into view, thereby setting an American Class B Closed Car Division record for the flying kilometer and mile. It was a remarkably calm beginning for a day that turned out, as do most speed record attempts, to be filled with high drama, short tempers and frantic action. Setting speed records is a unique business. It takes nerve, preparation, determination, skill and luck—and Mickey is no stranger to these elements.

Born in San Fernando, California, on Dec. 7, 1928, Thompson grew up in the midst of the thriving hot rod movement that flourishes in the California sunshine. From the moment he received his driver's license at 16, he was bent on record-breaking, pouring all his effort and money into cars for local dry lakes competition, Bonneville's famed Salt Flats and quarter-mile drag strips.

It was this frenzy of hot rodding and countless club speed records as an amateur that prepared him to seek his life-long goal, the World's Unlimited Speed Record. With his four-engined Challenger I, his first venture to bring him any measure of financial support from manufacturers, he set records in 1959 and 1960 for various distances, but fell short of the big one. He *did* become an uncrowned champion in 1960 when he exceeded the 394.2-mph record, driving 406.6 mph. It was, however, only a one-way speed and car failure made it impossible for him to set the required two-way average.

However, the fame gained from this run enabled him to leave his job as a newspaper color press operator and establish a thriving speed equipment manufacturing business in Long Beach, California, where he has ventured forth with assorted record cars, setting new marks in wholesale fashion, establishing himself as one of the giants in the world of speed. With his cars, constructed and tuned with hot rod know-how, Mickey has brought to this country records formerly held by such international stars as Rudolf Caracciola and Bernd Rosemeyer. Speeds set by the once-invincible Auto Unions have fallen to Thompson, as have records of Mercedes-Benz, Bugatti and Maserati.

His intent, that Sunday morning in California, was to raise his own standing kilo and mile records, and set new flying kilo and mile records in his stock car. With his tiny supercharged streamliner, "Attempt," he planned to capture international Class D standing kilo and mile records, a set of speeds which had eluded him one year earlier in a similar effort. He succeeded in all but the Class D mile mark.

He had been assured that there wasn't enough room on the March strip to set flying speeds, and there wasn't—on the strip. So he started about one-half mile past its north end, plunging across rough ground and through tall grass at impossible speeds before hitting the comparatively smooth pavement. It was very simple, except when he hit a dip on the strip and started to slide sideways at 150 mph. And at the south end he found himself bouncing across access roads, sailing 50 feet in one leap, ultimately running over some landing lights.

His first flying speeds, just over 149 mph, were good for a record but Mickey decided to try to do better later. He moved into the standing start records. Both these were his from the previous year; he raised them substantially and easily, the Pontiac sounding strong and sure as it pounded along the strip.

Then, time to try the streamliner. Essentially a dragster with a full envelope body, it is powered with a Pontiac

158

aluminum V-8, de-stroked to 180 cubic inches, developing about 500 hp at 7000 rpm. Here he found his first frustration. The drum of nitro turned out to be alcohol. While someone telephoned for the nitro to be delivered from Mickey's Long Beach shop 60 miles away, he tried the car on alcohol. As he was flagged away, someone stepped through the timing light, spoiling the timing tape on the run. But it didn't matter because the front-mounted supercharger scattered itself into small pieces part way along the course.

The problem had been anticipated. A top-mounted blower was pulled from the parts truck and mechanics prepared to install it. Such a job is no small task, and when it is important to do it rapidly, before heat and wind spoil chances of running, it becomes a monster. As they worked over it, nothing seemed to go right. The idler pulley wouldn't align, causing the blower drive belt to roll off. (This, remember, was a totally different blower location from the destroyed unit.)

Never one to waste a moment, Mickey climbed back into the stocker, taking another shot at the flying records he had set earlier. His second average was slightly worse than the first. But there was hope; his north-to-south run had been excellent—152.724. He could use it as long as he completed an opposite-direction run within one hour. At this point, wind was gusting against him and he didn't have as long a starting area for the required direction. He made one return run, turned around and stopped at the United States Auto Club timing trailer to get his speed. Not good enough. With seconds to spare, he swung back for another try. Just over 148 mph and barely within the time limit. He had raised his early-morning record.

Mickey's crew was still working with the streamliner and it was pushing 11 A.M., with temperature and breeze increasing. The blower mounting didn't look good, but Mick climbed in for a short sprint to see if the belt would hold. It did. He gave the order to put the body on. This required quick and ready work with tin snips to cut a ragged hole for the supercharger. The beautiful streamliner would never be the same.

He made his first run through the kilo. A safe but not comfortable margin of five mph over the old record of 110.2, set by Rudi Caracciola in a Mercedes-Benz in 1939. As the crew swarmed over the car, changing oil, plugs and water, Mickey announced that the course was so rough he had had double vision; he literally couldn't see where he was going

159

while hitting a terminal speed of about 235 mph. He was not pleased with the prospect of returning, but he had come this far . . .

His decision was to return at least through the kilo and if it was as rough as he knew it would be, he'd end the run there.

The car was ready. Mickey asked everyone watching to give him plenty of room—just in case. He started strongly, in the face of quartering headwinds. The car moved toward the kilo marker and, without warning, observers saw the parachute blossom about 200 feet *before* the end of the kilo. Mickey rolled to a stop, climbed out, thoroughly dejected. He explained that the engine had seized and the rear wheels had been locked for the last 500 feet of the run. He had opened the 'chute to retain control. With the shocking slowdown where he needed all the speed he could get, there seemed no chance for the record. And with a broken car he was finished for the day.

It was like the last-minute climax of a television western when USAC official Joe Petrali drove up with a broad smile and the news that Mickey's average of 112.088 had just squeaked past the old record. There was no denying it; Mickey had overridden an incredible set of circumstances and come out a winner. It was a day to remember in the history of speed, but it had been, as matters developed, just a brief, high-powered warm-up to the main event which began at Bonneville eight days later.

Mickey took two cars and a lot of hopes to the Utah salt flats. He planned to run his four-engined Challenger and capture the official World's Land Speed Record. He also had the March AFB stock car along, which turned out to be the machine that made the trip worth while.

His efforts at breaking 400 mph were over almost as soon as they began on Monday, July 25th. After announcing that he was retiring from land speed record driving at the end of the week, whether or not he achieved his goal, he climbed into Challenger I and made a painful discovery. His back, broken in a speedboat accident, would no longer bend to fit the contour of the seat as it had two years earlier. But he started the car on a trial run, driving away as spectators watched the Challenger bounce crazily across two miles of salt, a section which proved to be unusable. Mickey moved to a smoother area, turned around and gave the car a quick 300-mph blast that could have been disastrous. He had removed the canopy in order to better observe the car, and the wind speed was enough to split his goggles before he stopped. The car was right but the salt was not; there was only 9.6 good miles and Mickey needed more. The Challenger had made its last run.

The following day he moved to the stock car, setting a series of straightaway standing and flying records that wiped out two of his own speeds from the previous week. Next morning, just past dawn, he started driving the 10-mile circle, setting up lap speeds, along with co-driver Lloyd Cox, of just under 150 mph. The Pontiac ran strongly for most of 760 miles until a broken rocker arm stud forced the run's conclusion.

There had been no pre-determined goal for the circle runs; all depended upon the condition of the salt and how long the car would run. As the morning sun began to draw the moisture to the surface, sections of the salt became slushy. Pools of water appeared and holes were eroded, making parts of the circle as slippery as an ice rink. As each record fell to the storming Pontiac, Mickey determined to go to the next one. At 500 miles, he decided to push on to 1000 kilometers (621 miles), despite one weak cylinder which had reduced maximum engine revs to 5200. From 1000 kilos the next goal, never reached, was 1000 miles.

The list of records Thompson and Cox achieved was impressive, but there seems little doubt that they could have done better. The engine, running without air cleaners, was sucking salt into the cylinders. One observer termed it "a salt re-bore." Pit work was sometimes confused. There were two minor engine fires when oil was spilled onto the exhaust headers; refueling was sloppy and potentially dangerous. There were two flat tires, not the fault of the Goodyears, but caused by running on the black line, picking up surveyors' nails.

But all things considered, Thompson was satisfied. He may be all finished with 400-mph driving, but there are other records to be had, and he'll be back after them.

GO, MAN, GO!

by Randall Jarrell

If, by any remote chance, there are some readers of this book who consider automobiles to be no more than a means of getting from point A to point B, distressingly expensive creations of iron and rubber whose most important feature is that of reliability, then such readers are advised to turn to more practical volumes. Because here we celebrate cars. And who better to do the celebrating than Randall Jarrell, whose poetry has placed him in the front rank of America's *belles lettres?*

Come, Muse, let's sing of rats!" one eighteenth-century poem begins; the Department of Physical Education of one Midwestern university offers courses called "Beanbag I" and "Beanbag II." Writing on so insignificant a subject as sports cars makes me feel like a rat poet, a beanbag professor, and I have to reassure myself with Samuel Johnson's "Nothing is too insignificant for so insignificant a creature as man."

But part of me does not need reassuring; part of me, like part of you, feels, Cars, cars! Nor do we feel this simply because we are Americans. Alfa Romeo test drivers go at a hundred miles an hour through the streets of Milan while the pedestrians and the traffic policeman applaud; England has two prosperous weekly magazines in which ladies write lives of their 11-year-old Austins, and sports reporters tell by how many seconds a 30-year-old Bentley beat a 35-year-old Bugatti in a vintage race at Brighton. Cars are some of the things we share with the rest of the world, the rest of the ages: a man polishing his Mercedes is the last link in a chain that goes back to Achilles patting his divine steeds Balius and Xanthus—or, at least, that's what I tell myself as I polish my Mercedes.

People love cars. Looking at them driving off fast in every direction, a Thoreau or Emerson might ask: "From what are they all escaping?" The answer is, "Themselves"; if only they'd stayed home and cultivated those selves they wouldn't need to escape from them. "It is because our own eyes are so dull that the chromium on our cars shine so," the Thoreau or Emerson would continue. All this is one of those demeaning truths to which we say, "It's so. It's so," and walk away muttering, "Thank God *something* shines!" Nor should the word "escape" frighten us: most selves are good things to escape from—happy the man who has become, for a moment, selfless!

Proust says about people: No matter how ugly and old and odd you are, there is always someone whose ideal love you would be if only he could find you. It's true of cars. Steam cars, electrics like little parlors with cut-glass bud vases, touring cars ten feet high whose side curtains are of many-windowed isinglass, whose tops can be erected by three men in two hours and, once up, can shelter half a circus—you all have someone to bid for you shining-eyed, to take you home and, after many nights and many days, restore you to your original, authentic, mint condition. If we were like cars someone would marry us at the age of 40 for our patent leather fenders curved like a wave, our mahogany toolboxes, our gleaming brass lanterns and radiators and Motometers, our "mother-in-law seats" out in the open behind the rear wheels, our tires whose treads spell "Nonskid"; for the Russian fur coats and fur trousers and leather face masks in which our passengers rode in winter; for our varnished artillery-spoke wheels higher than a man's heart —four, six, eight of them. Yes, there *was* an Octoauto, and Elbert Hubbard was paid to say of it: "It is figured out on a reasonable basis that by the use of eight wheels eight times the ordinary service is obtainable."

Ah, advertisements of yesteryear! One could read, in 1910: "Protect your car against theft. Locks may be picked or jimmied. But no thief ever attempted to steal a car with a man at the wheel. Bosco's collapsible rubber driver is so lifelike and terrifying that nobody a foot away can tell it isn't a real, live man. When not in use, this marvelous device is simply deflated and put under the seat. Price $15."

These collapsible rubber drivers, like the real, live ones, are unrestorable; but the cars they drove still glitter in Glidden Tours or at antique car meets, where they look as improbably magnificent as old uniforms, engraved tournament armor. As loved, as collected are the classic cars: the Duesenbergs, Hispano-Suizas, Isotta Fraschinis, Mercedes,

163

Pierce-Arrows, Packards, Rolls-Royces, Bugattis of the twenties and thirties. Is stepping into *your* car "like stepping into a palace"? Does *your* car have a 180-inch wheel base; an engine four feet, seven inches long; a top speed of 140; a price of $30,000; a guarantee for the lifetime of the owner? The Bugatti Royale had them all.

In England they still race such cars. In Italy they race everything: 200-mile-an-hour Ferraris, jeeps, scooters, economy cars whose engine the mechanic lifts from the trunk with one hand. On dirt or asphalt ovals we Americans race stock cars, jalopies, midgets, one-man Indianapolis racers; out on dry lakes and salt flats the lakesters and streamliners go record-hunting; at the drag strips souped-up stock cars, home- or garage-made dragsters spend their Sundays seeing which can accelerate fastest.

At a *concours d'elegance* a car is judged for its beauty, authenticity, perfection of maintenance; your 1899 De Dion Bouton may be disqualified because it has a 1901 mudguard or because, when the judge ran his white-gloved finger along the underside of the axle, it came away stained with a butterfly's blood. In rallies you drive over some labyrinth of iced roads—or, in summer, over the Alps—at a required 41.5 mph, while your navigator sweats and figures; at a hill climb—well, you can imagine what people do at a hill climb. But unless you're Beatrix Potter I don't think you can imagine what they do at trials. Over little rivers, through marshes, up grassy hillsides and monolithic crags—stalling, miring down, balancing with front wheels in air, capsizing —go hippity-hop, hippity-hop, little bicycle-wheeled baby-buggy cars driven, mostly, by middle-aged couples: husbands with clear, sparkling eyes and round, rosy cheeks; wives lying across the hood to keep the car's nose down but still managing to look like Mopsy, Flopsy and Cottontail after they'd found good homes and a husband with a hobby. And behind, sober-faced, attentive, decorously applauding, as natural and unquestioning as the willows they stand or sit on shooting sticks among, are the watchers of the trials. Ah, England!

And, best of all, there are sports cars. The sports car driver—the enthusiast, as he calls himself—is someone whose eyes get starry whenever he sees a sign saying "Winding road"; he corners all day and then drifts off into that country where no road is straight. Speed is only speed; it is the curves and hills, up-shifts and down-shifts, motions made just fast enough and just small enough that transform the indifferent inhabitant of a car into Driver. A Driver wants a car light and low; wants big, well-cooled brakes, quick, precise steering; wants the kind of suspension and weight-distribution that will make the car absolutely stable—"rock-steady," the enthusiast says—on curves and at high speed; wants four or more gears; wants the car, generally, open or openable, so that as he drives along country lanes he's out among, down among weeds and rabbits and Nature; wants a rigid, compact car that handles like a racer—and is, consequently, the safest thing on the road. And he wants it beautiful; the enthusiast may not be able to tell Gothic from Romanesque, Soutine from Giotto, but he can talk for half an hour about the aesthetic inferiority of the TF to the TC.

Some sports cars are fast, some surprisingly slow; some are closed and luxurious, some as open and luxurious as an orange crate. A few of the most famous makers are Alfa Romeo, Mercedes, Ferrari, Lancia, Maserati, Jaguar. Aston Martin, Frazer Nash, OSCA, Bristol, Porsche, BMW; as these names are read out to the enthusiast, drums roll and in the distance the shining trumpets blow. And for every enthusiast with a sports car, sports cars, there are dozens with the wrong-sized pocketbook, the wrong-sized family and a '53 Ford; these buy the magazines, read the books, go to the races, daydream, dream.

Enthusiasts can be divided into two classes, those who say, "It corners like it was on rails," and those who say, "She corners as if she were on rails, old boy!" One of these last may even wear string gloves, leather-palmed, a Norfolk jacket and Sherlock Holmes hat—or as *he* would say, a deer-stalker; if he does, there is nothing you can do. All enthusiasts say that their cars do *an honest hundred* (*honest* as opposed to *indicated*—the average speedometer is 10 per cent fast); that closing the car's door is *like closing a bank vault* (usually this is an exaggeration, but in the case of my Mercedes it is almost literally true: if you'll come listen to me close my car door I'll come listen to you close your bank vault). All enthusiasts speak in approving or longing tones of things like overhead cams, knock-off hubs, sprung weight, oversquare engines, "light" or "positive" steering, independent suspension, dry sump lubrication, flat cornering, close-ratio gear-boxes, wire wheels. All look down their noses at automatic transmission, power steering, long wheel bases, unsprung weight, roll, L-head engines, chromium, overhang, "Detroit iron." If a sports car jars their teeth out they say: "It hath (*hath* because their teeth are gone) a *firm* ride,"

165

and they mourn the fact that it doesn't have the *classical,* the *coal-cart* ride of the sports cars of yesteryear.

Enthusiasts treasure even the squeal of the pig; one of their commoner phrases is, "What a note!" Racing cars or sports cars that mean business—are real bombs—ought, as the rpm's go up, to make a hard, screaming sound. A noise like tearing silk is particularly prized; Bugattis are famous for it. A car friend of mine wrote to Cook Laboratories proposing that they make a record of the sounds of loved and famous marques (you call a make a marque); as his wife and he, my wife and I sit comfortably drinking cocoa, we cry, "Listen to that TC!" or else with a "Say, what's that?" run out to the porch. Often it's a truck. I know about the Colonel's lady and Judy O'Grady, but why should trucks and sports cars sound the same?

About sports cars even a lot of learning goes a little way. You must learn—well, more than most people would ever want to learn. You must learn not to confuse a Nash-Healey with a Frazer-Nash, and Austin-Healey, with an Aston Martin. Don't mix up Delahayes, Delages, De Dions—a De Dion isn't even a car any more but a kind of rear axle, and you need to know what kind. As for Farinas; Pinin is the best contemporary car-designer, Nino is the racing-driver and Stabilimento isn't a man but an establishment—it makes bodies. You mustn't confuse initials: TC's, TD's and TF's are different—words can't express *how* different—MG's; these have nothing to do with AC's, nor with HRG's, nor with BMW's —Frazer-Nashes once were British BMW's, and EMW's are Soviet Zone BMW's, and . . . but surely you don't want me to go on.

Or if you do, read *Road & Track.* Fortunate the man who has several years of *Road & Track* stacked under the bed! In them there are articles about, pictures of sports car races, Grand Prix races, classic cars, the latest bodies from Ghia and Bertone and Vignale, the last special some mute inglorious Dr. Porsche has made in a friend's garage—these and Le Mans, the Targa Florio, the Nurburgring, Fangio and Moss and Gonzales, Kling, Trintignant, the Marquis de Portago: *all the live murmur of a summer's day,* as the poet says.

There is a bliss in stamp-collecting that only stamp collectors know. As the enthusiast sits at the stop light in his Grand Prix Bugatti, converted for road use by the addition of a couple of bicycle fenders, he gets a stare of wondering contempt from the engineer of the leviathan beside him, a stare that says, "Some car! It's the size of a coaster-wagon, it hasn't even got Hydramatic, in a year more it'll be old enough to vote. Why don't you wise to yourself and buy a real car?"

A few thousand of these stares and the enthusiast begins composing a look of his own. A friend of mine, a rhetorician and MG-owner from way back, once put the look into words, and the words went:

"Someday as your Cadillac Imperial drives you along the highway—the days when you drove it are long gone by— look down from your high window, your power-operated window, at the couple below you, there at the stop light. They are different from you, very different . . . and yet they look happy. You have a tail 12 feet long, with fins as high as their windshield; you have a trunk large enough to hold their little bug of a car and the tugs you use to park your own; you billow along on springs so custardy-smooth, tires so super-cushioning that you need power steering just to turn your steering wheel. You have acquired, to move you from place to place, a two-and-a-half-ton estate on wheels; here and there about your grounds, on the broad expanse of a deck or fender, one sees objects of art or utility, in finest chromium, placed there by the hand of a master landscape gardener. If Rousseau could see you he would scratch his fur hat and murmur: 'Man was born free, yet everywhere we see him in Cadillacs.'

"Why should every driver need a machine to shift gears for him? I need one about as much as I need a machine to eat strawberries for me. My MG has, just under my hand, a little black lever that goes from gear to gear like a Nuremberg egg the goblins have made for me on special order— and I'm in the gear I want to be in, not the one a mentally deficient mechanical brain has decided I'd be better off in. And when I want to go around a corner I don't need sea room and some sailors singing *Blow the Man Down* to haul away until the steering wheel's come full circle and the corner's negotiated—I move my hand six inches and we're in the next street. Curves? Hah! There *are* no curves in an MG!"

We used to have an MG. People laughed at us, but it was worth it. "It'd be a nice little car to collect eggs under the barn in," a farmerly man said to us at a stop light. We smiled up at him. "Look, Mother," a little boy said. "Don't point at the people in the car," his mother said. "It's not a car, it's an MG," he said. We smiled up at him.

Children would come to us and beg for rides—children love MG's; Schatzel, our dachshund, would come and jump up in the MG and hope. Other MG-drivers would wave to us, and we would wave to them; when, waking in the night, I'd hear the distant snarl of an MG shifting gears, I would know that out there in the darkness was somebody who wanted to wave to me.

We called our MG Little Teakettle—anyway, we called it that once—because of the noise it made at an honest 59 miles an hour: a sleepy bubbling sound, inexpressibly contenting. Ours was black, a classic black, but we'd painted the wheels and grille and dash a beautiful mermaid's-eye blue; people would look admiringly at it, though none so admiringly as we. When we would see an MG that had had nothing done to it we would shake our heads, sorrowing and say: "Stock."

Even in snowstorms the children would say, "Oh, no, let's take the MG"; the smaller would sit on a pillow over the racing brake, the larger would fit herself, segment by segment, into the well, and off we went, as happy as anchovies. Snow-covered expanses were always hard for us to resist; we'd drive over the abandoned golf course at the college, get stuck in snow-covered ditches and call to the girls sledding, who would come and push us out. And in summer, driving a few blocks to the beach, we've carried three grownups—one a grandmother—two children, a dachshund, two kittens named Jason and Medea, a picnic basket, an air mattress, a beach umbrella and an inner tube.

Now, of course, we have the Mercedes. Ours is a sports car; white, with red leather; so beautiful we still walk away from it backward. Imitate Phil Hill as you will: no wheel lifts. Drive onto the shoulder at 60: nothing happens. Leaning back in our leather arm-chairs, warmed, ventilated, serene, Mary and I sigh luxuriously. "Isn't it *nice* we have our beautiful car!" our little Beatrice sighs from the back seat—if seat it can be called; and Alleyne, fitted against her like a jigsaw puzzle, makes a loving, loyal, strangled sound.

When we got the car we bought four cases of Pilsner Urquell, the Only Genuine Pilsner; it'd hardly be right for the drivers of a Mercedes to drink domestic beer, do you think? I have a German general's leather overcoat I bought in Austria; it weighs 40 pounds and is warm as a summer blanket, and in it I look so—so lifelike and terrifying that a foot away nobody can tell it isn't a real, live general. When I wear it and Mary wears a Garbo- or lady-spy-type trench coat and we speed along, all sleek and white and low, with little Negro children calling to us, sweet as song sparrows, "Go, man, go!"—why, then we feel like Toad in *The Wind in the Willows* when he saw his first car; "Glorious, stirring sight! The poetry of motion! The *real* way to travel! Here today—in next week tomorrow! . . . And to think I never even *knew!* All those wasted years that lie behind me, I never knew, never even *dreamt!* That swan, that sunbeam, that thunderbolt!" And when we park our swan, our sunbeam, our thunderbolt, the passers-by go round and round it wide-eyed, open-mouthed, and ask us what it is, and we tell them. Only the other day a man came up to the car, and looked, and looked, and finally said: "Is that a homemade car?" After a minute my wife said no, and he said, turning to leave us: "There's a guy on the Burlington Road that makes cars like that for people."

We mean to keep it till we die. And yet we keep reading the used-car advertisements in the *Times* and *Road & Track* and *The Autocar:* we can't help thinking how nice it would be to have another Mercedes. A 300 SL, for instance, has fuel injection and gull-wing doors, and with a high-speed axle will do 167. It's not that I *want* to do 167, but it'd be a nice thing to have in reserve for Judgment Day. And 540 K's! They really are the classic car to end all classic cars—why, children could have a bobsled race down the front fenders, and the ignition keys weigh half a pound and look as if they'd been designed by Dürer for a drawbridge.

And—and we keep meeting our MG. It's had a wreck, and the left front fender's gone. It was the fault of the lady in the other car, and her insurance company is paying for a new fender, but just the same, we can't help thinking, *we'd* have dodged her. That poor rusty crumpled fender! Maybe we should have kept the MG—lots of families that hardly care about cars at all have two cars. If I had a 300 SL and Mary had the 190 SL and Alleyne—Alleyne's had a driving course and could have the 540 K—no, that wouldn't do, they didn't teach her to shift gears; but the MG would be just the right size for Beatrice, when she gets a little older and needs a car. And then there're the cats and Schatzel . . .

Cars, cars!